GW01071940

teach
yourself

windows xp

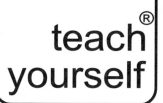

windows xp

mac bride

for over 60 years, more than 40
million people have learnt over
750 subjects the **teach yourself**
way, with impressive results.

be where you want to be with
teach yourself

For UK orders: please contact Bookpoint Ltd., 130 Milton Park, Abingdon, Oxon OX14 4SB. Telephone: +44 (0)/1235 827720. Fax: +44 (0)/1235 400454. Lines are open 09.00–18.00, Monday to Saturday, with a 24-hour message answering service. You can also order through our website www.madaboutbooks.com.

For USA order enquiries: please contact McGraw-Hill Customer Services, PO Box 545, Blacklick, OH 43004-0545, USA. Telephone: 1-800-722-4726. Fax: 1-614-755-5645.

For Canada order enquiries: please contact McGraw-Hill Ryerson Ltd., 300 Water St, Whitby, Ontario L1N 9B6, Canada. Telephone: 905 430 5000. Fax: 905 430 5020.

Long renowned as the authoritative source for self-guided learning – with more than 30 million copies sold worldwide – the *Teach Yourself* series includes over 300 titles in the fields of languages, crafts, hobbies, business, computing and education.

British Library Cataloguing in Publication Data
A catalogue record for this title is available from The British Library.

Library of Congress Catalog Card Number: On file.

First published in UK 2003 by Hodder Headline Plc., 338 Euston Road, London, NW1 3BH.

First published in US 2003 by Contemporary Books, A Division of The McGraw-Hill Companies, 1 Prudential Plaza, 130 East Randolph Street, Chicago, Illinois 60601 USA.

The 'Teach Yourself' name is a registered trade mark of Hodder & Stoughton Ltd. Computer hardware and software brand names mentioned in this book are protected by their respective trademarks and are acknowledged.

Copyright © 2003 Mac Bride

Typeset by MacDesign, Southampton
Printed in Great Britain for Hodder & Stoughton Educational, a division of Hodder Headline Plc, 338 Euston Road, London NW1 3BH by Cox & Wyman Ltd., Reading, Berkshire.

Impression number   10 9 8 7 6 5 4 3 2
Year   2007 2006 2005 2004 2003

contents

preface ix
01 introducing windows xp 1
1.1 What is Windows XP? 2
1.2 The Desktop 4
1.3 The mouse 7
1.4 The keyboard 8
1.5 Menus 9
1.6 The Start menu 11
1.7 Shortcut menus 12
1.8 Properties, dialog boxes and options 13
02 the desktop 17
2.1 Desktop Properties 18
2.2 Themes 18
2.3 The Background 19
2.4 The screen saver 22
2.5 Appearance 23
2.6 Settings 26
03 working with windows 28
3.1 Basic windows concepts 29
3.2 Using the scroll bars 32
3.3 Screen layouts 32
3.4 Tabbing between windows 35
3.5 Adjusting the window size 35
3.6 Moving windows 37
3.7 Closing windows 38
3.8 Turning off 38

preface

Windows XP is the latest version of Microsoft's world-beating operating system, and one that takes another step further along the path of making computers easier to use.

Teach Yourself Windows XP is written primarily for those who are new to computers, or are at least new to the Windows way – if you have previously used any reasonably modern version of Windows (95 or NT or later), the change to XP is very simple. This book introduces the basic concepts of working with Windows (the system) and windows (the framed parts of the screen in which programs run). It will show you how to set up your computer to suit the way you like to work – you can control more or less everything from the screen display down to the speed of the mouse's response! You will find out how to manage files efficiently, organizing your storage so that you can find things quickly and removing unwanted clutter, and how to care for your disks so they continue to perform well for a long time.

The Windows package includes many accessories and applications, both large and small. We will be looking briefly at some of these, and more closely at Internet Explorer and Outlook Express. With these two tools you can browse and download files from the Internet, and handle e-mail and newsgroup articles. Windows XP has been designed for easy Internet access, in fact, integration with the Internet is central to its design. If you choose, and if your hardware and connections are able to support it, you can almost treat the Internet as an extension of your desktop.

This book does not aim to cover every single aspect of Windows XP, for two very good reasons. There is far too much to fit into 250 pages, and few people will ever use all its features. *Teach Yourself Windows XP* concentrates on the needs of the new user at home and in the office. It aims to cover the things that you need to know to be able to use your computer efficiently, and things that you might like to know because they can make using your computer more enjoyable. Working with Windows is intuitive – once you know how to 'intuit'! When you have mastered the basics and become familiar with some applications, you should be able to apply your understanding of the 'Windows way' to any other Windows applications that interest you.

Happy Windowing.

Mac Bride

macbride@tcp.co.uk

2003

1

introducing windows xp

In this chapter you will learn

- the essentials of Windows
- about the Windows desktop
- about the mouse and the keyboard
- how to use menus
- how to set options

Aims of this chapter

Windows XP is very easy to use – once you have mastered a few key skills and concepts. This chapter gives an overview of Windows XP and of how it works. It looks at what you see on screen, and how you can respond to it and control it with the mouse and keyboard. It also introduces some essential terminology and the ideas behind them.

If you have previously used any similar computer system – such as Windows 95, NT or 3.1, or Apple Macintosh – you can skim through the next few pages, or skip them altogether, and go straight to Chapter 2.

1.1 What is Windows XP?

Windows XP is an *operating system* – and more. An operating system handles the low-level interaction between the processor and the screen, memory, mouse, disk drives, printer and other peripherals. Windows XP has *drivers* (control programs) for all PC-compatible processors and for many of the PC peripherals on the market – though some Windows 95/98 peripherals will not work with XP until their makers produce new drivers for them. The operating system is a bridge between the hardware of the computer and its *applications* – such as word-processors and spreadsheets. As a result, whatever hardware you are using, as long as it can run the Windows XP operating system, it can run any Windows XP application. (It will also be able to run applications written for earlier versions of Windows NT/2000 and most Windows 95/98 applications.)

Although the operating system is the most important part of Windows, most of it is invisible. You don't even need to think about how it works or what it does as Windows XP has its own routines for checking and maintaining the operating system.

Plug and Play

These built-in maintenance routines also come into play when you add new hardware, such as a joystick, scanner or extra hard drive, to your PC. Windows XP will normally recognize their presence automatically, and install the software needed to control them. The 'plug and play' approach makes it easy to add peripherals to your system.

The Desktop

The most visible part of Windows is, of course, the screen or *Desktop*. Windows is a graphical system. It uses *icons* (small images) to represent programs and files, and visual displays to show what is happening inside your PC. Many of the routine jobs are done by clicking on, dragging or otherwise manipulating these images, using the mouse or keyboard.

Windows is *multi-tasking* – it can run any number of programs at once. In practice, only a few will normally be active at the same time but that is more a reflection of the human inability to do several jobs simultaneously! A typical example of multi-tasking would be one program downloading material from the Internet and another printing a long report, while you wrote a letter in a third.

Each program runs in a separate area of the screen – a window – and these can be resized, moved, minimized or overlapped however you like. Managing windows is covered in Chapter 3.

Windows before XP

Up to now, there have been parallel Windows systems: Windows 3.1, followed by 95, then 98 and Me; and Windows NT, then 2000 for networked business users. Windows XP has been developed from the NT strand, so it enjoys its robustness, but adapted so that it can handle most existing Windows 95/98 applications – and many from earlier versions. Now all Windows users, whether at home or at work, on a stand-alone PC or a network, have the same system. (The only difference between the XP Professional and Home editions is that the Professional has a few extra facilities that could be useful to people on a large network.)

Utilities and accessories

Apart from the operating system, Windows XP contains a large set of programs. Some are utilities for managing the system –

organizing file storage on the disk, adding new peripherals or fine-tuning the way that they work. Others are applications for your use and amusement. You've got WordPad, a good word-processor, Paint for creating pictures and editing graphics, Movie Maker for editing home videos, a Calculator, some games, a set of multimedia tools and applications for the Internet, including Internet Explorer. All of the essential utilities and the more useful applications are covered in this book.

Integration with the Internet

Windows XP offers a high level of integration with the Internet – it can become almost an extension of your Desktop. Integration works best within organizations that are connected to the Internet through an ISDN line, giving fast, easy access – and preferably with the line open all the time.

If you connect through a dial-up line – as most home and small business users do – you cannot move smoothly from the Desktop to the Internet. In this situation, you will probably 'go online' (connect to the Internet) once or twice a day to get your e-mail or browse the Web, and this will be quite separate from your other computing activities.

Multiple users

Under Windows XP, a PC can be set up for multiple users (see section 8.7). Each user has their own file storage space on the hard disk and can customize the system to suit themselves.

1.2 The Desktop

The screen should be treated as if it really were a desktop. This is where you keep your tools – utilities and applications – and you can arrange things so that those tools you use most often are close at hand. This is where you create your documents – and you may have several under way at the same time, in the same or in separate applications. You can arrange these so that you can read two or more at once if you want to compare them or copy material from one to another. If you have finished with an application for the time being, you can tuck it out of the way – but it is ready to be restarted with a click of the mouse.

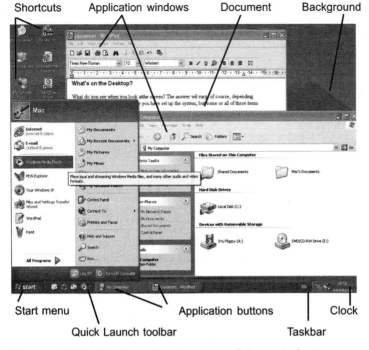

Shortcuts   Application windows   Document   Background

Start menu   Application buttons   Clock

Quick Launch toolbar   Taskbar

Figure 1.1 The Desktop showing some of the main features.

What's on the Desktop?

What do you see when you look at the screen? The answer will vary, of course, depending upon what you are doing and how you have set up the system, but some or all of these items should be visible.

Background

This may be a flat colour, a pattern, a picture or a Web page with text and images. It can be changed at any time without affecting anything else.

Shortcuts

These are icons with links to programs, to *folders* (for storing files on the hard disk) or to places on the Internet. Clicking on the icon will run the program, open the folder or take you off into the Internet. There are some shortcuts there already, but you can easily add your own (see page 93).

Taskbar

This is normally present as a strip along the bottom of the screen, but can be moved elsewhere (Chapter 9). It is the control centre for the Desktop, carrying the tools and buttons to start and to switch between applications.

Start menu

Clicking on the **Start** button opens the Start menu. Any application on your system can be run from here. The menu also leads to recently-used documents, the Help pages and other utilities.

Quick Launch toolbar

Shortcuts can be obscured by application windows, but the Taskbar is normally always visible. The Quick Launch toolbar is just one of the toolbars that can be added to the Taskbar to give you ready access to applications, no matter what the state of the Desktop.

Internet Explorer and Outlook Express are your main Internet applications (see Chapters 10 and 11). Media Player (section 14.6) plays a wide range of audio and video files. Show Desktop, shrinks all open applications out of the way so that you have a clear view of the Desktop.

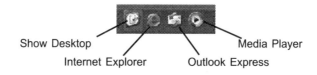

Show Desktop   Media Player

Internet Explorer   Outlook Express

Clock

This is optional, but useful. You should find that the clock keeps excellent time – it even adjusts itself at the start and end of Summer Time!

The Taskbar

The Quick Launch toolbar and Clock are covered along with the other Taskbar features, in Chapter 9.

Application windows

When you run an application, such as My Computer (Chapter 7), WordPad, or Paint (both in Chapter 14), it is displayed in a window. This can be set to fill the screen or to take a smaller area so that part of the Desktop is visible beneath (see Chapter 3 for more on windows).

Application buttons

When you run an application, a button is added to the Taskbar. Clicking on it will bring that application to the top of your Desktop.

Document

The letter that you are writing in WordPad, the picture in Paint, the budget you have set out in a spreadsheet – all of these are *documents*. A document is normally only seen in the application that created it, or a compatible one. In the screenshot on page 4, a document is open in WordPad.

> ### Customizing the Desktop
>
> The appearance of the Desktop and the way that you interact with it can be changed to suit yourself. See Chapter 2 to find out how to do this.

1.3 The mouse

The mouse is almost essential for work with Windows – you can manage without it, but not as easily. It is used for selecting and manipulating objects, highlighting text, making choices, and clicking icons and buttons – as well as drawing in graphics applications. There are five key 'moves'.

Point

The easy one! Move the mouse so that the tip of the arrow cursor (or the finger of the hand cursor) is over the object you want to point to. If you point to an icon, and hold the cursor there for a moment, a label will appear, telling you what the icon stands for. If you reach the edge of the mouse mat before the pointer has reached its target, pick the mouse up and put it down again in the middle of the mat.

Click

A single click of the left button will select an object or position the cursor in a block of text.

Right-click

A single click of the right button will open a shortcut menu (see page 11).

Double-click

Two clicks, in quick succession, of the left button will start a program or open a document. You can adjust the double-click speed (see page 122).

Drag

Point to an object or place on the Desktop, hold down the left mouse button and draw the cursor across the screen.

1.4 The keyboard

The keyboard is mainly for entering and editing text, but can also be used for controlling the system. These keys are worth identifying and noting:

Windows – press to open the Start menu.

Control – used in combination with other keys for shortcuts to menu commands.

Alt – mainly used for menu selections (page 9).

Application – acts like a right-click, displaying the shortcut menu of a selected item (page 11).

or The **Enter** keys, used after entering text or for selecting.

The first **Function** key. This one always calls up Help. The others do different jobs, depending upon the application.

Backspace – deletes the selected object on screen or the letter to the left in a block of text.

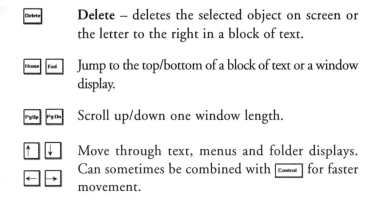

Delete – deletes the selected object on screen or the letter to the right in a block of text.

Jump to the top/bottom of a block of text or a window display.

Scroll up/down one window length.

Move through text, menus and folder displays. Can sometimes be combined with Control for faster movement.

1.5 Menus

In any Windows XP (or earlier) applications, the commands and options are grouped on a set of pull-down menus.

They follow simple rules:

* If an item has ▸ on the right, a submenu will open when you point to the item.

* If an item has … after the name, a panel or dialog box (page 13) will open when you point to the item.

* If an item has ● to its left, it is the selected option from a set.

* If an item has ✔ to its left, it is an option and is turned on – click to turn it off or on again.

* If a name is in grey ('greyed out'), the command is not available at that time – you probably have to select something first.

Menus and the mouse

* **To open a menu**: click on its name in the Menu bar.

* **To run a command or set an option**: click on it with the mouse.

* **To leave the menu system without selecting a command**: click anywhere else on the screen.

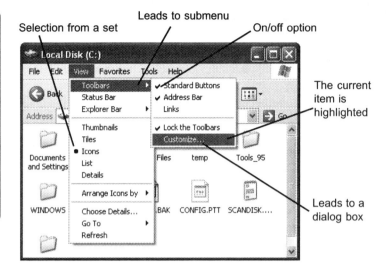

Leads to submenu

Selection from a set

On/off option

The current item is highlighted

Leads to a dialog box

Figure 1.2 A typical menu (this is in Windows Explorer).

Menu selection using the keyboard

When the work that you are doing is mainly typing, you may find it more convenient to make your menu selections via the keyboard.

To select from a menu with the keys:

1 Hold down **Alt** and press the underlined letter in the name on the Menu bar.

Either

2 Press the underlined letter of the name to run the command, set the on/off option or open the submenu.

Or

3 Move through the menus with the arrow keys – up/down the menu and right to open submenus – then press **Enter**.

◆ The left/right arrows will move you from one menu to another.

◆ Press the **Escape** key to close the menu without selecting a command.

Keyboard shortcuts

Many applications allow you to run some of the most commonly-used commands directly from the keyboard, without touching the menu system. For example, in Paint, **Control + S** (i.e. hold down the **Control** key and press **S**) will call up the **Save** command; **Control + O** has the same effect as selecting **Open** from the **File** menu.

The shortcuts vary, and some applications will offer far more than others, but some are common to all – or most – applications. If a command has a keyboard shortcut, it will be shown on the menu, to the right of the name.

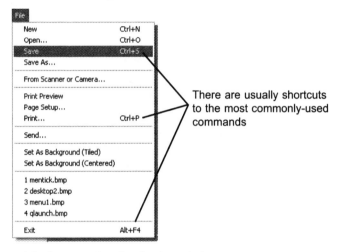

There are usually shortcuts to the most commonly-used commands

Figure 1.3 A menu showing keyboard shortcuts.

1.6 The Start menu

Any work that you want to do on your PC can be started from the Start menu – and many jobs can also be started from elsewhere, as you will see. The menu has been designed to give you quick access to things that you are likely to need most.

On the left are links to the six applications that you used most recently, with Internet and e-mail above; on the right are a set of key Windows facilities, and above these are links to folders where you probably keep your documents.

If you want an application that isn't listed on the left, clicking *All Programs* opens a menu through which every installed application can be reached.

We'll come back to the use of the Start menu in Chapter 5, and in Chapter 9 look at ways of customizing it to suit the way you like to work.

Figure 1.4 The Start menu as it first appears – you may have a different selection of application links on the left.

1.7 Shortcut menus

If you right-click on more or less anything on the screen, or press the **Application** key when an object is selected, a menu will appear beside or on the object. This is its *shortcut* or *context menu* – it will contain a set of commands and options that are relevant to the object in that context.

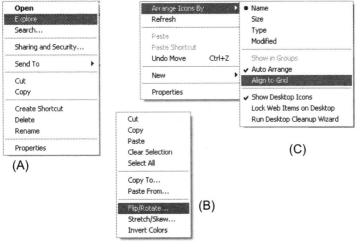

Figure 1.5 Three examples of shortcut menus, from (**A**) a folder in My Computer, (**B**) a selected area in Paint and (**C**) the Desktop.

Right-click on a shortcut to a folder, on a shortcut to an application, on the Taskbar or on the background and see what comes up. Don't worry at this stage about what the commands and options do, just notice how they vary – and that some are present on many menus.

1.8 Properties, dialog boxes and options

Almost every object in the Windows XP system has *Properties*, which define what it looks like and how it works. These can be seen, and often changed, through the Properties panel. This is normally reached through the context menu – you will see that two of the menus in Figure 1.5 have **Properties** as the last item.

Properties panels often have several *tabs*, each dealing with a different aspect of the object. The contents vary enormously. Some will simply contain information – such as the size, date and other details of a file – others have options that you can set in different ways.

♦ To switch between tabs, click on the name at the top.

Display Properties

Themes | Desktop | Screen Saver | Appearance | Settings

Click on the name to open a tab.

When you have finished with a panel, click **OK** to fix your changes, or **Cancel** to leave things as they were before. **Apply** will make the changes but leave the panel open.

Screen saver

Beziers | Settings | Preview

Wait 14 minutes ☑ On resume, display Welcome screen

Monitor power

To adjust monitor power settings and save energy, click Power.

Power...

OK | Cancel | Apply

Figure 1.6 The **Properties** panel from the Desktop (see Chapter 2). The tabs on some Properties panels are purely for information; these all have options that you can use to configure your Desktop.

When a Windows program wants to get information from you, it will do it through a *panel* or *dialog box*. These vary in size and style, depending upon the information to be collected.

Windows uses a range of methods for setting options and collecting information in its Properties panels and dialog boxes.

Text boxes

Typically used for collecting filenames or personal details. Sometimes a value will be suggested by the system. Edit it, or retype it if necessary.

Drop-down lists

These look like text boxes but have an arrow (🔽 or 🔽) to their right. Click on the arrow to make the list drop down, then select a value.

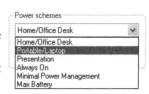

Power schemes

Home/Office Desk

Home/Office Desk
Portable/Laptop
Presentation
Always On
Minimal Power Management
Max Battery

Drop-down list (open) – select from the list

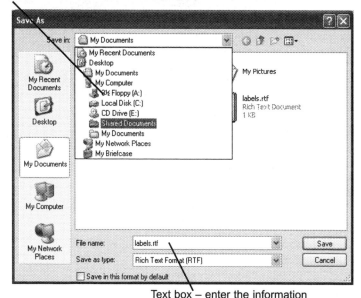

Text box – enter the information

Figure 1.7 A **Save As** dialog box with an open drop-down list and a text box. The **Save as type** options are also on a drop-down list.

Lists

With a simple list, just scroll through it and select a value. They sometimes have a linked text box. The selected value is displayed there, but you can also type in a value.

Check boxes

These are switches for options – click to turn them on or off. Check boxes are sometimes found singly, but often in sets. You can have any number of check boxes on at the same time, unlike radio buttons.

Radio buttons

These are used to select one – and only one – from a set of alternatives. Click on the button or its name to select.

Sliders and number values

Sliders are used where an approximate value will do – for example, volume controls, speed and colour definition (actual values may not mean much to most of us in these situations!). Clicking to the side of the slider will move it towards the click point, or you can drag the slider in the required direction.

Numbers are often set through scroll boxes. Click the up or down arrows to adjust the value. If you want to make a big change, type in a new value.

Summary

- ◆ Windows XP is an operating system with a package of utilities and application programs.

- ◆ The screen is referred to as the Desktop, and should be treated much as a real desktop.

- ◆ The mouse responds to single and double clicks of the left button, and to single clicks of the right button. It can also be used to drag objects across the Desktop.

- ◆ Certain keys serve specific functions.

- ◆ In any application, the commands can be reached through the menu system.

- ◆ Some commands have keyboard shortcuts.

- ◆ The Start menu gives you quick ways to start work.

- ◆ Right-clicking on an object normally opens a shortcut menu, containing relevant commands.

- ◆ Windows XP has a number of simple ways to set options and make selections.

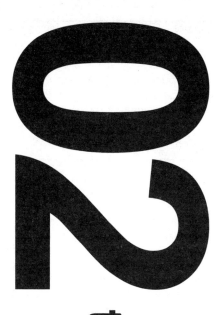

02

the desktop

In this chapter you will learn

- about the Desktop
- how to change the theme and the background
- about screen savers
- how to customize the appearance
- about the display settings

Aims of this chapter

In this chapter we will look at the Desktop itself, and ways to arrange items on it – experimenting will show you what works best for you in different situations. We will also look at how you can change the appearance of the Desktop, as you should set the screen up to suit yourself before you go any further into your explorations of Windows XP.

2.1 Desktop Properties

The Desktop display options are to be found on its Properties panel, or on dialog boxes that open from there. There are five tabs, and a lot of options. You can change the background image, the colour and fonts used for windows, menus, dialog boxes and similar components, the screen saver, and the size of the display. You may well not want to tackle all of them at one sitting, but that's not a problem. You can change any of the settings whenever you like, and as often as you like. If several people use the PC, and user accounts (see page 125) have been set up for each, then they can all have their own Desktop settings which will be applied when they log on.

Feel free to experiment – it's your Desktop.

*   To open the **Properties** panel, right-click anywhere on the Desktop and select **Properties** from the menu.

2.2 Themes

A theme sets the overall style for the Desktop – its background image, the icons for the standard Windows utilities, the selection of colours and fonts, and the sounds that are triggered by events (alerts, prompts, startup and shut down, etc.). You don't have to accept the whole theme – if there are parts you don't like, you can modify them on the other tabs. For example, the Jungle theme has quite a lush, though dark, background and entertaining icons, but the default fonts are hard to read. These can be changed from the Appearance tab.

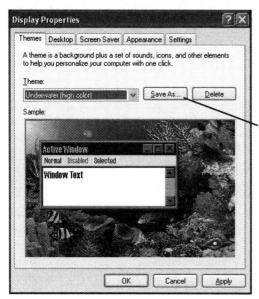

If you modify a theme, you can save it with a new name. This will let you change themes, but return to your carefully modified one at a later date.

Figure 2.1 The **Themes** tab.

1 The Properties panel should open at the **Themes** tab, if it doesn't click on the tab label to open it.

2 Click the down arrow to open the **Themes** list, and select a theme. It will be previewed in the **Sample** pane.

3 When you find one that you like, click **Apply** to fix it before you move to the other tabs to tweak its appearance.

2.3 The Background

Click the **Desktop** tab on the **Display Properties** panel to get to this.

The background is purely decorative! The background can be a plain colour, a single picture, a small image 'tiled' to fill the whole screen or an HTML document. Windows XP has a selection of small and large images, but any JPG, GIF or BMP image or even a Web page can be used.

1 Scroll through the list of images and pages. If you find one that seems interesting, select it to see its preview.

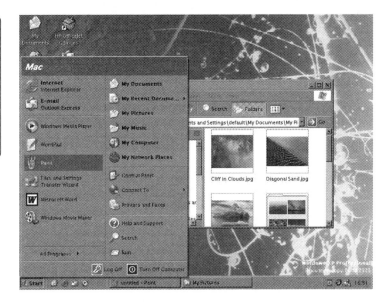

Figure 2.2 The same screen, but different themes. Note how the theme has an impact on just about every part of the display.

- With a small image, set the **Display** mode to **Tile**. The image will be repeated across and down to fill the screen.

- With a larger image, set the **Display** mode to **Center** to see it in its natural size, or **Stretch** to make it fill the screen.

2 Click **Apply** to test your selection. If you don't like it, try another.

*Don't click **OK** yet. If you do, it will close the Display Properties panel and we have not finished exploring it.*

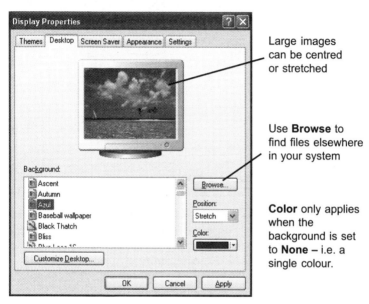

Large images can be centred or stretched

Use **Browse** to find files elsewhere in your system

Color only applies when the background is set to **None** – i.e. a single colour.

Figure 2.3 The **Desktop** tab – there is a good selection of background pictures, but you can just as easily use one of your own.

Customizing the Desktop

While you are on the Desktop tab, click the **Customize Desktop** button. This opens the **Desktop Items** panel.

On the **General** tab you can toggle the display of the icons for My Documents, My Computer, My Network Places and Internet Explorer. Turn off those that you do not use. You can also select new images for the standard icons, and – rather more usefully – you can run the Desktop Cleanup Wizard. This will

Turn this on if you want the Wizard to run automatically every 60 days

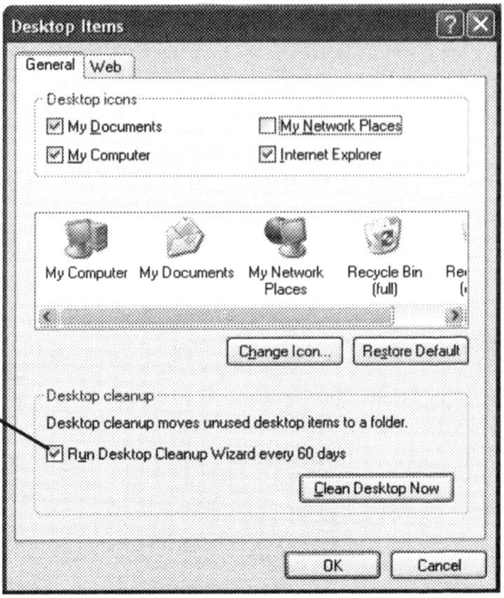

Figure 2.4 The **General** tab of the Desktop Items dialog box.

pick up any icons that you have not used for a long while and tuck them into an *Unused Items* folder on the Desktop.

On the Web tab, you can link to a Web page to make that the background image. I suspect that this is probably only likely to be of interest to people who have permanently open lines to the Web and who need up-to-the-minute information from a specialist service.

2.4 The screen saver

This is mainly decorative. A screen saver is a moving image that takes over the screen if the computer is left unattended for a while. On older monitors this prevented a static image from burning a permanent ghost image into the screen. Newer monitors do not suffer from this, and in fact, most now have an energy saving feature that turns them off when they are not in use. If your monitor has this, the screen saver will only be visible briefly, if at all.

A screen saver can be password protected (or revert to the log-on screen where there are several users), so that it will lock the system until the password is entered. This can be useful if you do not want passers-by to read your screen while you are away from your desk.

How long does the computer have to be idle before the Screen Saver should kick in?

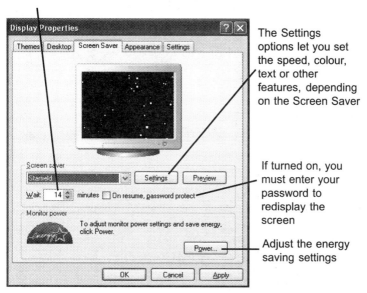

The Settings options let you set the speed, colour, text or other features, depending on the Screen Saver

If turned on, you must enter your password to redisplay the screen

Adjust the energy saving settings

Figure 2.5 The **Screen Saver** tab. Click the **Power...** button to set the times that the system should wait before shutting down the monitor and the hard drive. Don't make these waits too short. Turning a monitor on and off constantly may well reduce its lifespan.

2.5 Appearance

Use this panel to set the style, colour and fonts for the Desktop and standard Windows-elements in all applications – the menus, dialog boxes, etc.

The main option here is on the **Windows and buttons** drop-down list. You display them in one of two styles:

● *Windows XP Style*, which gives you a very limited choice of colour schemes;

• *Windows Classic Style*, which gives you a very wide range of colour schemes, including several high contrast schemes for the visually impaired.

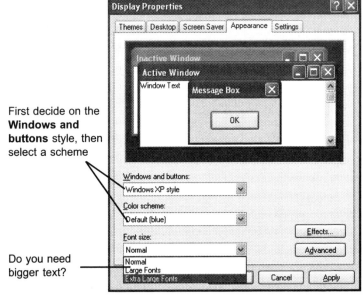

First decide on the **Windows and buttons** style, then select a scheme

Do you need bigger text?

Figure 2.6 The **Appearance** tab.

Whichever scheme you choose, you can adjust the size, colour and font of individual screen elements through the **Advanced** dialog box.

1 Click the **Advanced** button to open the dialog box.

2 Click on an item in the preview pane, or select it from the Item drop-down list.

3 Set its size and colour, and font attributes as required.

4 Click **OK** to return to the **Properties** panel.

Effects

The **Effects** dialog box, reached from the **Effects** button on the Appearance tab, contains only one significant option – turn on **Use large icons** if you need the extra visibility. The other options are largely decorative.

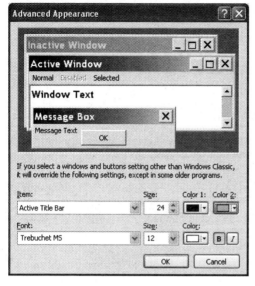

Only some items
have the full range
of colour and font
options

Figure 2.7 The **Advanced Appearance** dialog box.

Most of these
options are just
for show – and all
take processing
power. If you
want the system
to run at top
speed, turn them
all off.

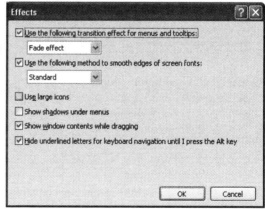

Figure 2.8 The **Effects** dialog box – if you do not need large icons,
ignore this one.

2.6 Settings

The Settings relate to the size of the screen and number of colours used in the display. They should normally be left at their defaults as Windows XP will select the optimum settings for your system – and the Advanced settings should certainly be left alone unless you know and understand the details of your system. Bad selections here can really mess up your screen!

The Screen resolution is set fairly low here as this works better for the (small) pictures I need for this book. 1280 by 1024 pixels or higher makes better use of a 19" monitor

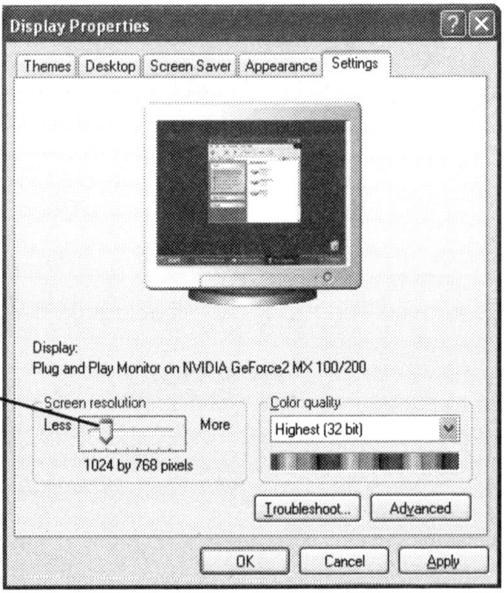

Figure 2.9 The **Settings** tab.

Save your theme

It can take a while to get everything 'just so', and it would be a shame to lose all that hard work if at some point you switch to another theme. When you have finished setting options, click the **Save As...** button on the Themes tab and save the settings as a theme. If you, or someone else, later changes the settings, you can get your desktop back by selecting your saved theme.

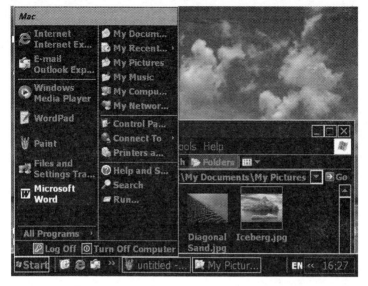

Figure 2.10 One of the **High Contrast schemes** from the Classic set, with large fonts. For maximum visibility, try the High Contrast White, with extra large fonts.

Summary

- The Desktop Properties control its appearance.

- The choice of theme sets the overall style of the Desktop.

- Many aspects of the screen can be controlled through the Display properties panel.

- The Background and Screen Saver options are largely decorative and have little impact on the working of your system.

- The Appearance options can be set to high contrast and large fonts if you need to make the display easier to see.

03 working with windows

In this chapter you will learn

- how to control windows
- how to scroll around in a window
- about screen layout
- how to move between windows
- how to close programs and exit Windows XP safely

Aims of this chapter

If you only use one application at a time, you don't have to think too much about managing windows – there will only be the one. But this kind of usage does not take advantage of Windows XP, a multi-tasking system. If you want to have several applications open, you must know how to switch between them, and how to arrange their windows so that you can work efficiently. This chapter will show you how.

3.1 Basic windows concepts

A window is a self-contained, framed area of the screen that is controlled independently of any other windows. All applications are displayed in windows. If an application can handle multiple documents, they may each be displayed in their own window within the application.

All windows have these features:

• **Title bar** showing the name of the application or document;

• **Minimize, Maximize** and **Close** buttons on the far right of the title bar – for changing the mode (page 30) and for shutting down;

• An icon at the far left of the Title Bar – leading to the window's **Control menu** (page 31);

• **Scroll bars** along the right and bottom – for moving the contents within the frame. These are only present if the contents are too wide or too long to fit within the frame.

• A thin outer **border** – for changing the window size (page 35).

Application windows also have:

• **Menu bar** – leading to the application's full set of commands and options;

• One or more **Toolbars** – containing icons that call up the more commonly-used commands and options. Toolbars are normally along the top of the working area, but may be down either side, or as 'floating' panels anywhere on screen.

• The **Status bar** – displaying a variety of information about the current activity in the application.

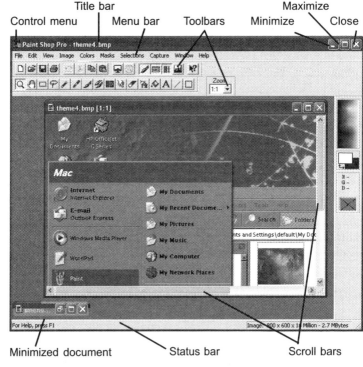

Figure 3.1 The main features of windows.

Both application and document windows can be in one of three modes, and the simplest way to switch them is with the buttons at the top right:

Maximize – An application window fills the screen and loses its outer frame. When a document is maximized in its application's working area, its Title bar is merged with the application Title bar and its window control buttons are placed on the far right of the Menu bar.

Minimize – An application is then visible only as a button on the Taskbar. A minimized document is reduced so that only the Title bar and window control buttons are visible.

Restore – The window is smaller than the full screen or working area. Its size can be adjusted, and it can be moved to any position – within or beyond the limits of the screen.

Restore is on the **Maximize** button in a maximized window, and on the **Minimize** button of a minimized window.

The Control menu

This is opened by clicking the icon at the far left of the Title bar. But this is really here for keyboard users.

Press **Alt** and the **Space bar** to open the menu in applications, or **Alt** and the **Minus** key in documents.

You can now Mi<u>n</u>imize, Ma<u>x</u>imize/<u>R</u>estore or <u>C</u>lose by pressing the keys of the underlined letters. (**Alt + F4** is a shortcut for Close.)

This is also where keyboard users start to <u>M</u>ove (page 37) or change the <u>S</u>ize (page 35) of the window.

How many windows at once?

There is no fixed limit to the number of windows that you can have open at the same time. The maximum depends on the amount of RAM on the computer and how memory-hungry the applications are. You won't run many big programs at once in a 64Mb machine, but 128Mb should be able to handle far more than you could ever realistically want.

I once had 30 applications running simultaneously, though 26 of these were started accidentally! (Tip: don't lean on the **Enter** key when an application icon is selected on the Desktop...)

3.2 Using the scroll bars

When you are working on a large picture or a long document, only the part that you are working on is displayed within the window. Scroll bars will be present along the bottom and/or right of the frame and can be used to move the hidden parts of the document into the working area. They can be controlled in three ways:

♦ Click on the arrows at the ends to nudge the contents in the direction of the arrow – typically the movement will be a line or so at a time, but the amount of movement varies with the application and document size.

♦ Click on the bar to the side of or above or below the slider for a larger movement – typically just less than the height or width of the working area.

♦ Drag the slider. This is the quickest way to scroll through a large document.

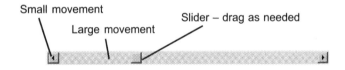

Small movement

Large movement

Slider – drag as needed

Automatic scrolling

If the typing, drawing or other movements that you make while working on your document take the current position out of the visible area, the document will be scrolled automatically to bring the current position back into view.

3.3 Screen layouts

Windows XP allows you enormous flexibility in your screen layouts, though the simplest layout that will do the job is usually the best. You can only ever work on one application at a time – though you can copy or move files or data between two windows and there may be continuing activities, such as printing or downloading, going on in other windows. If you do not

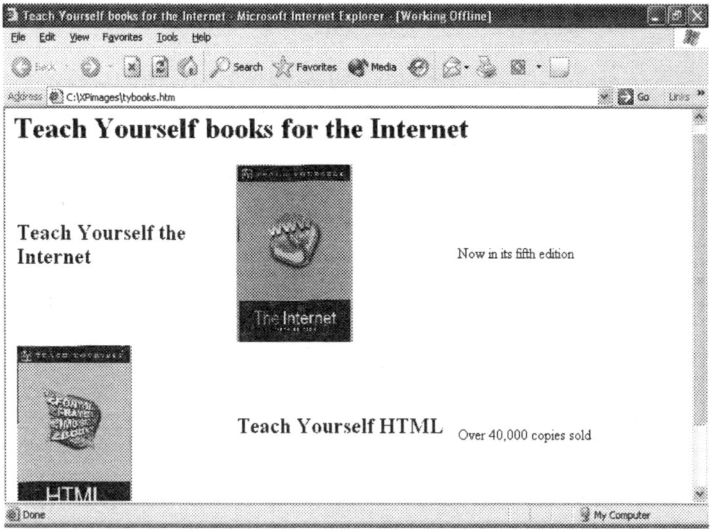

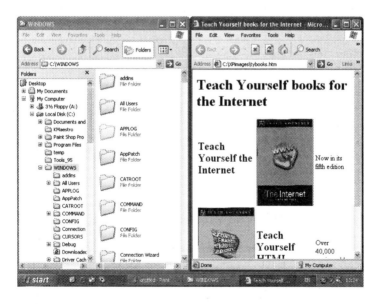

Figure 3.2 If you are only using one application, run it in a Maximized window for the largest working/viewing area.

Figure 3.3 The **Tile** displays work better with bigger screens. An 800 by 600 pixel screen can only handle two windows comfortably.

actually need to see what is happening in the other windows, the simplest layout is to run all applications in Maximized mode. The one that you are working on will fill the screen, obscuring the others, but you can easily bring one of those to the front by clicking on its button in the Taskbar.

The Windows key and Taskbar buttons

If you don't want to use the mouse to click the Taskbar buttons, hold down the **Windows** key and press **Tab**. This will select one of the Taskbar buttons – keep pressing **Tab** to move between the buttons. When the one you want is selected, press **Enter** to activate its window.

Multiple window layouts

Sometimes you will want to be able to see two or more windows at the same time – perhaps to copy material from one application to another or to copy or move files. The simplest approach here is to use the **Cascade** and **Tile** commands. They will take all windows currently open in Maximized or Restore mode and arrange them overlapping (**Cascade**), side-by-side (**Tile Horizontally**) or one above the other (**Tile Vertically**).

1 Check that all the windows you want to include in the display are in Maximized or Restore mode.

2 Right-click on a blank area of the Taskbar.

3 Select the **Cascade** or **Tile Horizontally/Vertically** command.

4 When you want to return to the previous layout, right-click the Taskbar again. The menu will now have an **Undo Cascade** or **Undo Tile** command.

3.4 Tabbing between windows

Switching between windows by using their Taskbar buttons is not always convenient. However, there are a couple of neat alternatives. This is the one I prefer:

1 Hold down the **Alt** key and press **Tab**. This panel appears.

2 Press **Tab** again until the application that you want is high-lighted – if you go off the end, it cycles back to the start.

3 Release the **Alt** key.

The second alternative is to hold **Alt** and press **Escape**. That switches between windows and can be repeated until the right one is at the front of the Desktop.

3.5 Adjusting the window size

When a window is in Restore mode, its size can be adjusted freely. This can be done easily with the mouse or – less easily – with the keyboard.

To adjust the window size with the mouse:

1 Select the document or application window.

2 Point to an edge or corner of the frame – when you are in a suitable place the cursor changes to a double-headed arrow.

3 Hold down the left mouse button and drag an edge or a corner to change the window size. If the **Show windows contents while dragging** option is on, the window will change size as you drag. If it is off, you will see a shaded outline showing the new window size. (Set the option on the **Effects** button of the **Appearance** tab of the **Display Properties** dialog box, see page 24.)

4 Release the mouse button.

5 Repeat on other edges or corners if necessary.

To adjust the window size with the keyboard:

1 Open the Control menu by holding down **Alt** and pressing the **Space bar** (application) or pressing **Alt + minus** (document).

2 Press **S** to select Size.

3 Press the arrow key corresponding to the edge that you want to move. A double-headed arrow will appear on that edge.

4 Use the arrow keys to move the edge into its new position.

5 Press **Enter** to fix the new size.

6 Repeat for the other edges or corners if necessary.

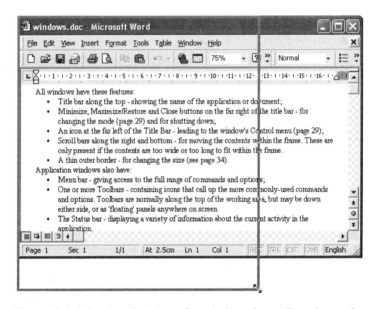

Figure 3.4 Adjusting the size of a window. An outline shows the new size as the *Show windows contents while dragging* option has been turned off. It can be more efficient to change the size by dragging a corner, rather than an edge, but it is trickier to locate the cursor at the start.

3.6 Moving windows

A window in Restore mode can be moved to anywhere on – or partly off – the screen (or within the working area in an application). The Title bar is the 'handle' for movement.

To move a window with the mouse:

◆ Point to anywhere on the Title bar and drag the window into its new place.

To move a window with the keyboard:

1 Open the Control menu and select **Move**.
2 Use the arrow keys to move the window as required.
3 Press **Enter** to fix the new position.

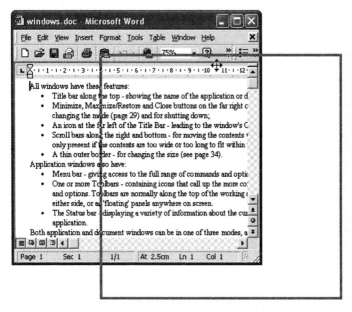

Figure 3.5 Moving a window. The 4-way arrow only appears when you start from the **Move** command in the Control menu. If *Show windows contents while dragging* is turned off, only the outline moves while you drag – the window then leaps into place when you release the mouse button.

3.7 Closing windows

When you have finished with a window, close it. This will free up memory so that other applications run more smoothly, as well as reducing the clutter on your Desktop. There are three methods which will work with any window:

◆ Click the **Close** button  in the top right corner.

◆ Hold down **Alt** and press the **minus** key to open the Control menu and select **Close**.

◆ Hold down the **Alt** key and press **F4**.

You can also close a window by exiting from an application (see *Closing programs*, page 66).

3.8 Turning off

When you have finished a working session, you must shut down the system properly – *do not simply turn off the PC*. Windows runs through a shutdown routine that removes any temporary files that were created by the system or by applications, checks the system and closes down safely. If you simply switch off, it may take longer than usual to restart, as Windows will need to check – and possibly restore – essential system files. It may even insist on starting in 'Safe mode' and perform a thorough check there before allowing you to start up properly.

To shut down Windows XP:

1 Click **Start** and select **Turn off Computer**. If any windows are open, they will be closed, and you may be prompted to save documents (page 66).

Or

Hold down the **Alt** key and press **F4** – if a window is open, the action will close that, and you will have to press **Alt + F4** again to shut down.

2 Select **Shut down**.

3 Wait a few moments until the PC turns itself off, or you are told that it is safe to turn it off.

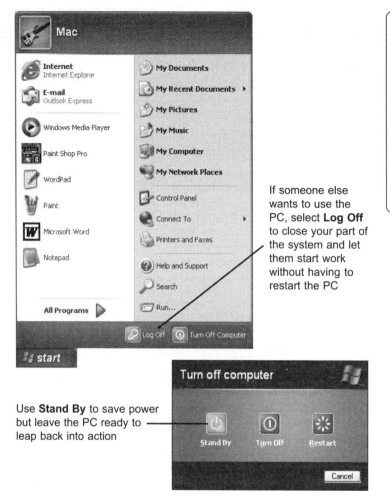

If someone else wants to use the PC, select **Log Off** to close your part of the system and let them start work without having to restart the PC

Use **Stand By** to save power but leave the PC ready to leap back into action

Figure 3.6 Turning off properly – don't just switch off!

Alternative endings

* Some PCs have a **Suspend**, **Stand By** or **Hibernate** mode which shuts down the screen and hard drive, but leaves the memory intact. While suspended, the power consumption is virtually nil, but the computer can be restarted almost instantly. This is an attractive alternative to a full shut down.

- If you have had an application crash or freeze up on you, a **Restart** will normally restore order, though on very rare occasions you may need a full shut down and power-off to recover. (See page 67 for more on this.)

If you are on a network or there are several user accounts (see page 125) on the PC, you should log off at the end of a session. Select **Log Off** on the Start menu and then...

- Click **Log Off** at the prompt. This shuts any open programs, but leaves the PC running, for you or another user to use later.

- Click **Switch User** at the prompt. This leaves your programs suspended, but allows another user to log in. It doesn't matter if they use the same programs as you have been using – the documents that you were working on will not (normally) be affected by anything they do. (The only possible problems you may have will occur if the other users try to work on documents that you have left open.) When they are finished you can log in again and pick up where you left off.

Figure 3.7 Select Switch User to leave your programs suspended while someone else uses the machine, or Log Off if you have done for the day.

Summary

- Windows can be open in Maximized, Restore or Minimized modes.

- To switch between the display modes, use the control buttons on the top right of the frame, or the commands on the Control menu.

- If the contents of a window go beyond the boundaries of the frame, the Scroll bars can be used to pull distant areas into view.

- There are many different ways to arrange windows on your screen – the simplest is to work with all windows Maximized, pulling them to the front as needed.

- The Cascade and Tile arrangements will display all Maximized and Restore mode windows.

- You can switch between open windows by holding down Alt and pressing Tab.

- The size of a window can be changed by dragging on an edge or corner, or using the Control menu Size command and the arrow keys.

- Windows can be moved by dragging on their Title bar, or with the Control menu Move command.

- You must turn off properly, or log off, at the end of a session.

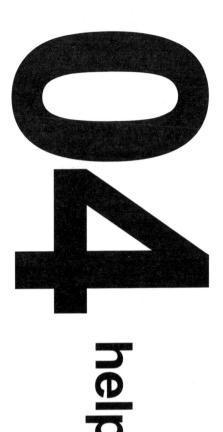

04 help!

In this chapter you will learn

- about the Help system
- how to use Help and Support
- how to search for help
- how to get help with tools and in dialog boxes
- how to use wizards

Aims of this chapter

If you ever get stuck while using Windows, there's plenty of help at hand. Windows XP has its own extensive Help and Support system with 'tours', 'tutorials' and interactive trouble-shooters, and every Windows application has its own Help system.

In this chapter you will learn how to navigate through these Help systems to find the assistance that you need. You will also see how to make good use of the other forms of Help that Windows XP offers.

4.1 Help and Support

The main Windows XP Help system is reached through the **Help and Support** item on the **Start** menu.

* Click **Start**, select **Help and Support** and you are in.

The Home Page

On the left of the Home page is a set of major topic headings. Each of these leads to a contents list for the topic, and here you will find three types of links.

☐ beside a heading shows that this will open a list of sub-topic links in the right pane – and clicking on one of these will display a page of Help.

⊞ indicates a group of headings – click to reveal the ☐ headings.

☒ is used for *See also* links to the glossary, list of keyboard shortcuts, tools and related newsgroups.

The Help pages assist in several ways. **Overviews, articles and tutorials** offer explanations or demonstrations of concepts or techniques; **Fix a problem** or **Pick a task** links will usually take you step-by-step through the use of a Windows utility – such as the Backup or Restore Wizard (page 202); some **Fix a problem** links lead to *troubleshooters*, which can be a real help in analysing why something won't work, and then fixing it.

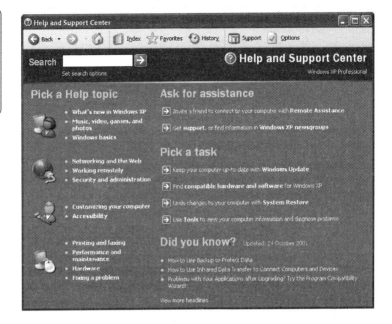

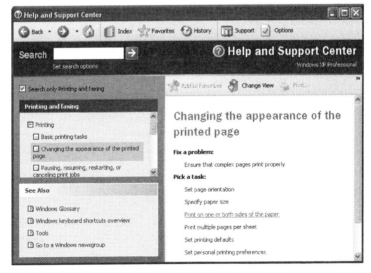

Figure 4.1 Picking a Help topic at the Home page of Help and Support opens a list of headings, each of which leads to a list of sub-topic links – click on these to display their Help pages.

Within a Help page, if a word is in green and underlined, then clicking on it will open a pop-up box giving a definition.

At the bottom of a Help page, you will normally find the label 'Related topics'. Click on this to open a short list of links to closely related topics.

Once you are into the Help pages, click:

◆ Back ▾ and ➤ ▾ to move between pages that you opened earlier, or

◆ to return to the Home page to explore a new topic.

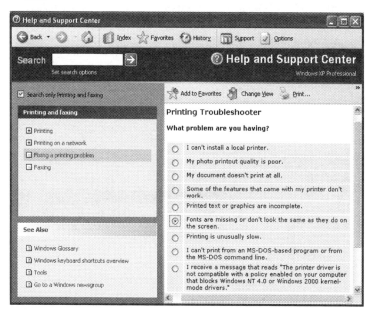

Figure 4.2 Troubleshooters can be very useful, especially when you are having difficulties with printers or peripherals. They will take you through a series of checks to diagnose – and often cure – problems.

The Index

To switch to the Index, click on its label in the menu bar. This works like the index of a book. To look up a word:

◆ Drag on the slider or click the down arrow to scroll through the list.

Or

1 Start to type the word in the top box. As you type, the system will leap through to the words that begin with the typed letters.

2 Pick a topic from the list and click [Display].

3 If there are several Help pages for the same index entry, you will be offered a choice – pick one and click [Display].

The Help pages that you find here are the same as those linked from the Home page.

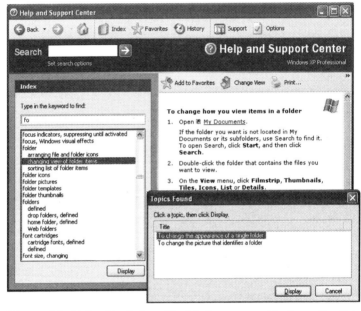

Figure 4.3 Using the Index. Start to type a word to focus the list, then select an index entry – some lead to several topics.

Search

The **Search** box is present on every page of the Help system. To run a search, type your keyword into the box and click ➡. The results are grouped in three sets – click the headers to see their results:

♦ **Suggested Topics** are normally the most useful. These are the pages that have been indexed by the keyword.

- **Full-text Search Matches** are pages which contain your keywords, but these may only be passing references.
- **Microsoft Knowledge Base** draws Help from Microsoft's Web site and is, of course, only available if you are online.

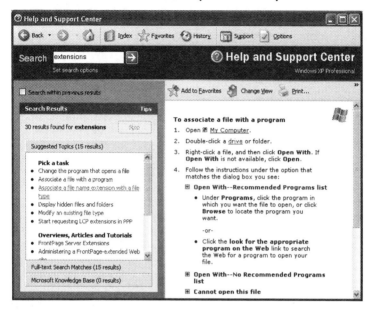

Figure 4.4 A Search can be started from any page of the Help system. Just type what you are looking for and click the arrow.

Keywords

When searching here – or on the Internet – a 'keyword' is simply a word that describes what you are looking for. If a word does not give you what you want, try a different word.

Change View

On the header bar of the Help topic display you will see **Change View**. If you click on this, the surrounding Help and Support window will close down, leaving just the topic display. This can be very useful if you want to keep the information visible while you tackle that tricky job.

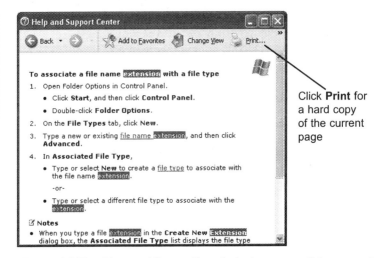

Back • | Add to Favorites | Change View | Print... »

To associate a file name extension with a file type

1. Open Folder Options in Control Panel.
   - Click **Start**, and then click **Control Panel**.
   - Double-click **Folder Options**.
2. On the **File Types** tab, click **New**.
3. Type a new or existing file name extension, and then click **Advanced**.
4. In **Associated File Type**,
   - Type or select **New** to create a file type to associate with the file name extension.
     -or-
   - Type or select a different file type to associate with the extension.

☑ **Notes**
- When you type a file extension in the **Create New Extension** dialog box, the **Associated File Type** list displays the file type

Click **Print** for a hard copy of the current page

Figure 4.5 The **Change View** option shuts down everything except the topic display. Remember that this is a window and can be resized to show more of the entry and/or moved to a convenient part of the screen so that you can still read it while working on whatever you needed Help on.

◆ Click [Change View] to reopen the full window if you need it.

Favorites and History

The Help system is made up of pages written using HTML – the same language that is used to create pages for the World Wide Web – so it is no surprise to see Favorites and History here. They are used in exactly the same way as they are in Internet Explorer, and if you haven't used that, then either go now to page 155 or leave these two Help features until after you have found your way around Internet Explorer.

Online support

The Help system offers three types of online support, and none of them are for the faint-hearted.

◆ **Ask a friend to help** lets you connect to a knowledgeable and sympathetic friend through the Messenger system (this lets you exchange messages with other Messenger-using friends and tells you which are online when you are). You can then talk about the problem with your friend who can view your screen and even operate your PC through the Internet. That's the theory. I'd be interested to see how it works out in practice. Drop me an e-mail if you've tried it!

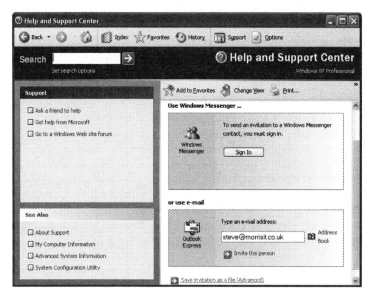

Figure 4.6 You can ask a friend to help – if you have a willing and able friend who also has XP and uses Messenger.

- **Get help from Microsoft** takes you to their technical support area on the Web. This is a very useful service for the technically minded but can be heavy going for the rest of us.

- The **Go to a Windows Web site forum** link takes you to newsgroups where XP is discussed. These can be good resources, particularly for more experienced users, but even new users may get some help here. For more on newsgroups, see page 190.

4.2 Application Help

The utilities and applications that are supplied as part of Windows XP – and other Windows applications from Microsoft or any software producer – also have their own Help systems. These all use the same standard approach which looks different from, but behaves in much the same way as the Help and Support system of Windows XP.

Look at the Menu bar in any application and you will see **Help** on the right. The first item on this menu is **Help Topics** or **Contents and Index**. Whatever the label, the first item is the way into the Help system.

Contents

A Help system can be thought of as a book, with a different topic on every page – though, unlike paper books, the pages vary in length. Related topics are arranged into chapters, and the whole book is extensively indexed. But this is a reference

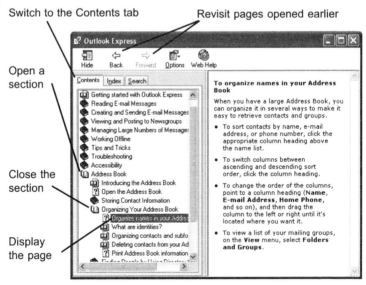

Figure 4.7 Outlook Express's Help, open at the Contents tab.

book. Don't attempt to read it all from start to finish, you'll just give yourself a headache.

The Help system normally opens at the **Contents** tab – if another tab is at the front, click on the **Contents** label to switch to it. Use this tab to get an overview of the available Help, and when you want to read around a topic. Initially, only the main section names will be visible.

+ Beside each section name is a 📖 icon. Click on the section name or the icon to open the section.

+ Some sections have subsections. Again, click on the name or 📖 to open one.

+ When you see a list of topic pages, click on the name or ▯ icon to display a page in the right-hand panel of the window.

+ Only one section is open at a time – the open one will close when you select another. If you want to close a section so that you can reach those that are off-screen, click the 📖 icon.

+ As you browse through the system, the **Back** and **Forwards** buttons become active, allowing you to return to pages that you have opened earlier in that session.

The Help pages contain descriptions of what things are and how they work, with instructions on how to perform tasks. The pages (both in Windows XP and in the latest applications) are written in HTML – HyperText Markup Language – the same coding system that is used for creating Web pages.

You will find that some text is underlined and 'hyperlinked' – point to it and the cursor changes to 🖑. Click and one of three things will happen:

+ If the text is <u>Click here to...</u>, a Wizard or an application will start.

+ If the text is <u>Related Topics</u>, either you will be shown a list of relevant pages from which you can pick one, or you will be taken directly to the related page if only one is available.

+ If the text is a <u>special term</u>, a panel will appear giving a definition of the term. Click anywhere at all to close the panel.

Index

The **Index** tab in application Help systems is very similar to that of Help and Support. Use it in just the same way.

1   Start to type a keyword into the text box at the top. The list will scroll to bring into view the words that start with those letters.

2   If the word you want is not yet visible, type more letters.

3   Select an entry or sub-entry from the list and click [Display].

4   If the entry leads to several Help pages, you will see the **Topics Found** list – select one from here and click [Display].

Type the first letter(s) of the word   Select an entry

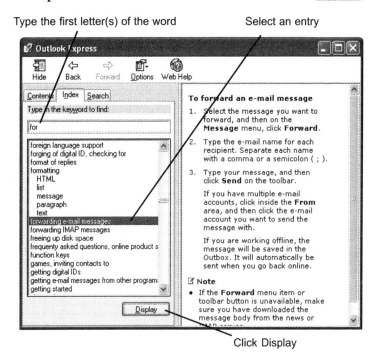

Click Display

Figure 4.8 Using the **Index** tab.

Creating the Index

The first time that you use the Index, you must wait for a moment while the system scans the Help pages to create it.

Search

Like the Index, Search uses keywords to find pages – but there is a crucial difference between them. The Index is created from selected words, and the entries are grouped by topic. In contrast, the Search is based on a full-text search of all the Help pages. As a result, a Search will find all pages that contain any given word, while the Index will only find those that had merited an index entry. Depending upon how well the Help is indexed, a Search can sometimes be far more productive than using the Index.

1 Switch to the **Search** tab.

2 Type one or more keywords into the text box.

3 Press **Enter** or click [List Topics].

4 Select a Topic from the list and click [Display].

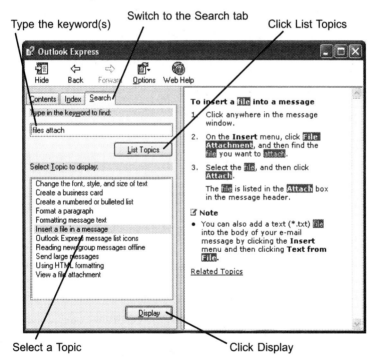

Type the keyword(s) Switch to the Search tab Click List Topics

Select a Topic Click Display

Figure 4.9 Using the **Search** tab. The keywords are normally highlighted wherever they occur in the page.

53 help! 04

Tools and options

The Help system has a small set of tools and options, which should give you all the control you need – most of the time you will probably go into Help, find and read a page or two, and come straight out again.

 Shuts the tab area, leaving just the page display – use it if you want to see more of the window beneath while you read the Help page. The icon then changes to **Show** – click this when you want to restore the tabs to view.

Figure 4.10 If you want to see more of the screen beneath while you are reading the Help pages, hide the tabs, and resize the window.

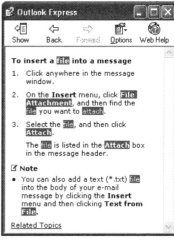

 Reopens the Help page opened before the current one (if any) during the session.

 Used after a **Back** move, to return to the next Help page in the sequence of those opened during the session.

 Most of the **Options** duplicate the tools, but note:

Refresh If you click on an underlined term for the definition or resize the window, the screen may not redisplay correctly afterwards. This will tidy it up.

Print Sends the current page to the printer.

Search Highlight On/Off Controls the highlighting of matching words in the pages found by a Search.

If you are online, this will connect to the Microsoft site where you can get Help with more advanced features or with technical problems. We will look at the Internet in Chapter 10.

4.3 Tips and prompts

Tooltips

The icons on tool buttons are generally good *reminders* of the nature of the tool, but they are not always immediately obvious to the new user. Tooltips are little pop-up labels that tell you what icons stand for.

Wait a moment for the Tooltip

Figure 4.11 If you don't know what an icon does, point to it and wait a second. A Tooltip will appear, giving its name. If you still need Help with it, at least you now know what to look up in the Index.

Status bar prompts

The Status bar serves many purposes – it is through here that applications will communicate with you, so do keep an eye on it. One of the uses is to display a brief description of items as you point to them in the menus.

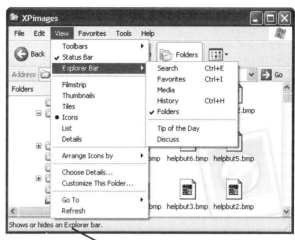

The Status bar tells you about menu items

Figure 4.12 When you point to an entry in a menu, a brief description appears in the Status bar at the bottom of the window.

Dialog box Help

If you look in the top right corner of dialog boxes and panels, you will normally see a ? button. You can use this to get brief explanations of the options, buttons and other features in the dialog box.

Here's how to get Help in a dialog box:

1 Click ?. The cursor changes to ?.

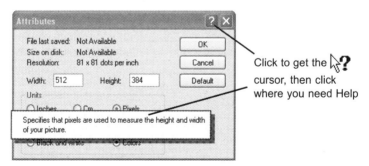

Click to get the ? cursor, then click where you need Help

Figure 4.13 When you first use a new dialog box, it's good to be able to get explanations of its options and features.

2 Click on the item that you do not understand. A panel will open, displaying an explanation of the item.

3 Click again – anywhere – to close the explanation panel.

4.4 Wizards

The Wizards are not part of the Help system, but they play an important role in making Windows easy to use. As a general rule, if you have hardware or software to set up – especially if it is a lengthy or tricky operation – there will be a Wizard to help you through it. All Wizards run in much the same way. You will see a series of panels. Each will ask you to set options or provide some information, and will give you guidance on how you should respond.

At the bottom of the panel are three buttons:

< Back Takes you back a step so that you can review or change options set at that stage.

Next > Takes you on to the next panel. When you reach the final panel, this is replaced by Finish .

Cancel Closes the Wizard, abandoning any settings you have made up to that point.

Figure 4.14 A typical panel from a Wizard – this one will help you to back up your files. (For more on this, see Chapter 12.)

The Cancel button is more useful than you might think. There will be times when you get part way through a Wizard and realize that you do not have the information that you need to complete the operation.

Summary

Windows XP tries to be user-friendly and to provide Help where it is needed.

* You can get into Windows' Help and Support system from the option on the Start menu.

* To browse through Help and Support, pick a topic from the headings on the Home page.

* To find Help and Support on a specific topic, use the Index section or run a Search.

* Troubleshooters can be very helpful in analysing and solving problems.

* Additional Help is available online, through links in the Support area.

* The Help systems in applications look different from Windows' Help and Support but are used in much the same way. Browse through the Contents or track down specific help through the Index or Search tabs.

* Tooltips and Status bar prompts can help you to get to grips with the tools and commands in a new application.

* The ? icon will give you explanations of the features of dialog boxes and panels.

* There are Wizards to help you with most configuration tasks.

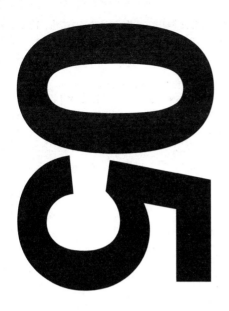

05

programs and documents

In this chapter you will learn

- about types of programs, applications and documents
- how to start a program
- how to open a document
- how to cope with crashes
- how to save files

Aims of this chapter

The whole purpose of Windows XP is, of course, to run applications and produce documents – almost everything in the system is concerned directly or indirectly with doing this. So, it's about time that we had a look at how to run applications, and how applications and documents are interrelated.

5.1 Definitions

Program

A program is a set of instructions, that make the computer perform a task. The task may be very simple, or highly complex. It is useful to divide programs into three types:

Operating system level programs

These are run and controlled by Windows XP – which is itself a program (or rather a set of interlinked programs). You are only aware of them by their effect. They manage the screen, pick up your keystrokes and mouse movements, control the transfer of data to and from the disk drives, prepare documents for output to the printer, and similar chores. Those of us who cut our computing teeth on older operating systems sometimes regret that Windows takes such total control of these, but overall it must be admitted that Windows does a very good job of management.

Utilities

These are the programs that you can use to manage your PC. Windows Explorer and My Computer, for example, allow you to organize your file storage (Chapter 7). There are programs in the Control Panel (Chapter 8) which you can use to customize the hardware and software, and another set that enable you to keep your disks in good order (Chapter 12).

Applications

These are why you use computers. They include business applications such as word-processors, spreadsheets, databases and accounts packages; graphics software for creating images;

browsers and other tools for communicating and working co-operatively on the Internet and on local networks; multimedia viewers, players and editing software; games and much else. Most, though not all applications, will produce or display documents, and any given application can only handle documents of a certain type or range of types. We'll return to this after one last definition.

Document

A document is an organized set of information produced by an application. It can be stored on disk as a file and – typically but not always – can be output onto paper, to be read or viewed away from the computer. Some obvious examples of documents are letters, essays and reports created on word-processors, but databases, spreadsheets and Web pages are also documents, as are images, sound and video files. When a document is saved, part of its name identifies the application that created it. This association with applications is central to the way that Windows handles documents. We will return to it in section 5.7.

5.2 Start ➡ All Programs

The simplest way to start an application or utility program is through the **Start** menu. Almost all of the programs now on your PC, and any that you install later, should have an entry in the **All Programs** part of the menu.

What's ➡ this?

In this book, ➡ is used to link the steps in a menu sequence, e.g. **Start ➡ All Programs ➡ Accessories** means 'select **Start** and from its menu pick **All Programs** then pick **Accessories**'.

A program may be on the first level of this menu, or may have been grouped onto a submenu – which may open up to a further level of submenus. The routines that install Windows XP and new software will create the Start menu entries and organize them into submenus, but if you do not like the structure, you can tailor it to suit yourself (see Chapter 9).

To start a program:

1 Click [*start*] or press [⊞] on your keyboard.

2 Point to **Programs**.

3 Click once on a program name.

Or

4 Point to a group name to open the next level of menu – and again if necessary – then select from there.

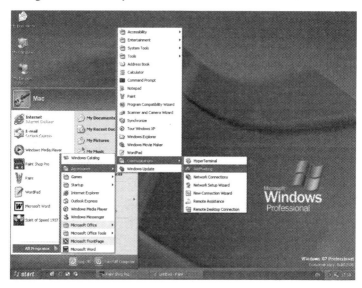

Figure 5.1 Starting from the Start menu. In this case, the program, **Net Meeting**, was on the third level of submenus. Notice **Windows Explorer** on the **Accessories** menu – you'll be needing that shortly! Notice also the Desktop Shortcuts in the background. These give quick access to regularly-used programs and folders.

5.3 Other ways to start

Explorer/My Computer

Windows Explorer and My Computer are the standard Windows XP file and folder management applications. The two do the same job in very similar ways, with very similar screen displays. We will be looking closely at these in Chapter 7. At this point it is worth noting that programs can be started from within them.

1   Open the folder containing the program file.

2   Click (or double-click) on the program name to start it.

Figure 5.2 Programs can be run from **Explorer** or **My Computer**, though it may sometimes take a while to find them!

Why start from Explorer or My Computer?

Not all programs have Start menu entries. For example, when you download software from the Internet, it is often in the form of a self-extracting Zip file – compressed and stored in an executable file (i.e. a program). When this is run, it extracts the software and installs it onto your system, normally creating Start menu entries so that you can run the new software. But that initial downloaded file will not have a menu entry. To run it, you will have to find it on your disk and run it through Explorer or My Computer.

Desktop Shortcuts

Shortcuts offer a quick route to regularly-used folders and programs. When you first start using Windows XP, you will find a dozen of these icons on the Desktop. Some, such as *My Documents*, lead to folders – click on these and My Computer will run, open at the selected folder. Others, such as the Internet

Explorer icon, lead to applications – click on these to start the application.

Over time you may want to add more shortcuts to favourite applications. This can be done easily through either Explorer or My Computer (see Chapter 7).

Taskbar toolbars

Initially, there is only one of these on the Taskbar, and that is the Quick Launch toolbar (page 5). It contains shortcuts to Internet Explorer, Outlook Express and Media Player, as well as 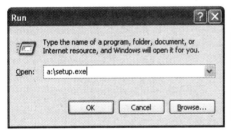 **Show Desktop**, which sets all open windows to Minimize, clearing the Desktop. Other toolbars can be added – you can even create your own if you like this way of starting applications (see Chapter 9).

Start ➡ Run

The first item on the right of the Start menu is **Run....** Click on this and a small panel opens. Here you can type a command line to start a program.

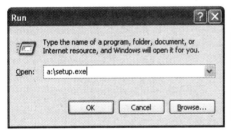

The **Run** panel being used to start an installation program from the A: drive. If Run is not present on your Start menu, it can be turned on in the Customize dialog box (see page 142).

The command line must include the path – the route from the drive through the folders and subfolders to reach the one containing the program, e.g. \WINZIP\WINZIP.EXE. If the program is not on the C: drive, the line must start with the drive letter (e.g. A: for the floppy and D: for the CD-ROM).

There are two situations in which you may want to use the Run approach to starting a program:

*   If you are installing software from a floppy disk or CD-ROM, there will usually be an installation program (typically called SETUP.EXE). To start this, type the drive letter,

then the path if necessary, followed by the program name, e.g. A:\SETUP.EXE.

Remember that you can also use Explorer or My Computer to locate and start these installation programs.

* Some old MS-DOS programs have start-up options which you can set by typing them into the command line. If you do come across such a program, the start-up options will normally be explained in a README file.

5.4 Starting from documents

Every type of document is – or can be – linked to an application (see *File Types*, section 7.6), so that when you open a document, Windows will run the appropriate application for you. Those that you have been working on recently can be opened from the **My Recent Documents** folder on the Start menu.

Figure 5.3 My Start menu – yours will adapt to suit your usage.

1 Click on **Start**.

2 Point to **My Recent Documents**. Its submenu contains shortcuts to your most recently used documents.

3 Select a document to run the linked application and open the document.

♦ Documents can also be opened from Windows Explorer or My Computer (see Chapter 7).

Documents from the Web

Internet Explorer also uses the File Types links – if it meets a file that it cannot handle, it opens the linked application to display the document (see Chapter 10).

5.5 Closing programs

When you have finished using an application, it must be closed down properly. Closing its window (page 38) will close the program, but you will also find a **Close** or **Exit** option on the **File** menu.

If you have created a new file or edited an old one, and not saved the changes, you will be prompted to save before the application closes.

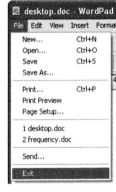

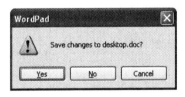

♦ Select **Yes** to save the file.
♦ Select **No** to exit without saving.
♦ Select **Cancel** to return to the application.

5.6 Coping with crashes

Windows XP is more reliable and robust than earlier versions of Windows, but software is rarely perfect. Some applications – and in particular some combinations of applications – are more likely than others to crash. If you are interested, crashes are normally caused by two programs trying to use the same area of memory, and you can go find a big technical book if you want to know more! If you are lucky, you won't have crashes often. But just in case...

Symptoms

One or more of:

- The busy symbol ⧗ appears and stays (but wait twice as long as normal just in case it has a lot more to do than you thought).

- No response to key presses or mouse actions.

- The screen does not display properly – there might be part of a window or dialog box left behind and unmovable.

Figure 5.4 The **Task Manager** dialog box (see page 68).

Solution

* Hold down **Ctrl** and **Alt**, and press **Delete**. The **Task Manager** dialog box will appear. Open the **Applications** tab if it is not already open. The program that has crashed should be at the top of the list – with 'not responding' after the name.

* If it is an application that is not responding, click **End Task** – you will be asked to confirm that you really want to close it. The system should work properly once it is out of the way.

* If the highlighted program is *not* marked '(not responding)', it probably hasn't crashed – click **Cancel** and give Windows a bit longer to sort itself out.

5.7 Filenames and extensions

When documents are saved onto disk, they are given a name which has two parts. The first part identifies that particular document, and can be more or less anything you want (see *Rules for filenames*, below). The second part is a three-letter extension which identifies the type of document. This is normally set by the application in which the document is created, and it is through this that Windows can link documents and applications. (We'll look at how to create links in section 7.6.)

Here are some extensions that you are likely to meet:

.TXT   Simple text, without any formatting or styling

.DOC   Word document

.HTM   Web page – can be created by many applications

.BMP   bitmap image, e.g. from Paint

.GIF   a standard format for images on Web pages

.JPG   an alternative format for Web page images

.EXE   an executable program – not a document!

.PDF   Portable Document Format – used for creating formatted documents that can be read on any computer (as long as it has the free Acrobat Reader software)

.RTF   Rich Text Format – used to transfer formatted text between applications.

Rules for filenames

The first part of the name can be as long as you like (up to 250 characters!) and can consist of any combination of letters, numbers, spaces and underlines, but no other symbols.

It's common sense to make sure that the name means something to you, so that you can easily identify the file when you come back to it later – and the shorter the name, the smaller the chance of making a mistake if you have to type it again.

The extension must match the application. As a general rule, when you save a file for the first time, simply give the identifying name and let the application set the extension. If the application can output documents in different formats, and you know that you need a particular format, select it from the **Save as type** list. After the first save, the filename is set, though the file could be later saved under a different name and in a different format. You might, for example, have written a report in Word, but want to give a copy to a colleague who used WordPerfect.

Standard formats

Life would be easier if there was only one standard format for each type of document, but instead there are loads of them, especially for word-processing and graphics. You might wonder why. According to the old joke, computer people love standards – which is why they have so many.

In fact, there are several reasons. When a software house develops a new application, or a new version of an existing one, it will normally use a different document format – partly to handle its special features, and partly to distinguish it from its rivals. Some formats are developed to meet particular needs. With graphics documents, for instance, there is a trade-off between file size and image quality, and formats have been developed across the range.

Figure 5.5 A typical **Save As** dialog box. This one is from a graphics package, and can save in several standard formats. All applications have their own 'native' format, and many can also import or export documents in other formats for use with other applications. Word 2002, for example, can open or save documents as plain text, Web pages, Rich Text Format files, Excel spreadsheets(!), WordPerfect, Works, Write or several earlier versions of Word.

Summary

+ There are three main types of programs: those run by the operating system, utilities for managing your computer, and applications for doing useful work or having fun!

+ The data files produced by or displayed by applications are known as documents.

- Programs can be set running from the Start menu, Desktop Shortcuts, the Taskbar, the Run dialog box or from within Explorer or My Computer.

- Opening a document in the My Recent Documents menu or in Explorer or My Computer will run its associated application.

- Programs should be closed down properly when you have finished using them.

- If a program crashes and hangs the system, the **Ctrl** + **Alt** + **Delete** key combination will open the Task Manager dialog box. You should be able to close the offending program from here.

- Documents are given filenames when they are saved onto disk. These have two parts: the first part is simply an identifying name and can be more or less anything you like; the second part describes the format of the file and is usually set by the application in which it was created.

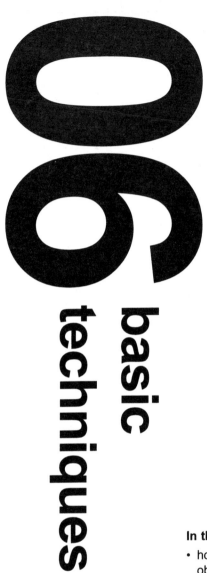

06 basic techniques

In this chapter you will learn

- how to select text and objects
- how to Cut, Copy and Paste
- about the Clipboard
- how to use drag and drop
- about Desktop scraps

Aims of this chapter

One of the great attractions of Windows is consistency. Every Windows application will have a similar basic layout and tackle the same jobs in much the same way. As a result, once you have learnt how to use one Windows application, you are well on the way to knowing how to use any other. This chapter looks at some of the basic techniques for working with Windows – selecting objects, moving objects on screen and copying through the Clipboard and through 'scraps'.

6.1 Selection techniques

Before you can do any work on an object or a set of objects – e.g. format a block of text, copy part of an image, move a group of files from one folder to another – you must select it.

Text

Use WordPad or any word-processor to try out these techniques. They can also be used with text objects in graphics packages and even with small items of text such as filenames.

To select with the mouse:

1 Point to the start of the text.

2 Hold down the left mouse button and drag across the screen.

3 The selected text will be highlighted.

To select with the keyboard:

1 Move the cursor to the start of the text.

2 Hold down the **Shift** key.

3 Use the arrow keys to highlight the text you want.

Graphics

The same techniques are used for images in graphics applications, and for icons on the Desktop, files in My Computer and other screen objects.

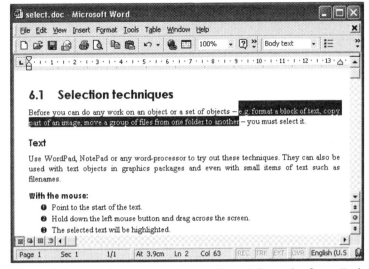

Figure 6.1 Once the text has been selected, it can be formatted, deleted, copied or moved.

To select a single object:

◆ Point to it. If this does not highlight it, click on it.

To select adjacent objects:

1 Imagine a rectangle that will enclose the objects.

2 Point to one corner of this rectangle.

3 Hold down the left mouse button and drag across to the opposite corner – an outline will appear as you do this.

Or

4 Select the object at one corner.

5 Hold down **Shift** and select the object at the opposite corner.

To select scattered objects:

1 Highlight the first object.

2 Hold down the **Ctrl** key and highlight each object in turn.

3 If you select an object by mistake, point to (or click on) it again to remove the highlighting.

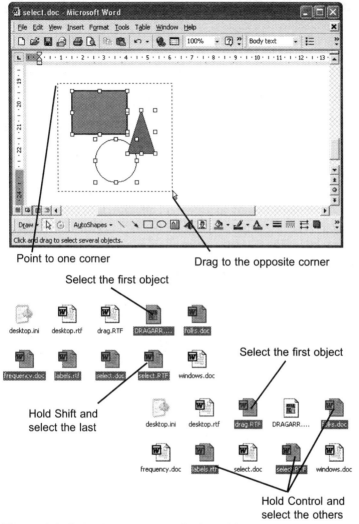

Point to one corner

Drag to the opposite corner

Select the first object

Select the first object

Hold Shift and
select the last

Hold Control and
select the others

Figure 6.2 Selecting images and other objects.

Deleting objects

All applications have a Delete command (usually on the
Edit menu), but selected objects can also be deleted by
pressing [Delete] or [←]. Use these with care!!

6.2 Cut, Copy and Paste

If you look at the Edit menu of any Windows application, you will find the commands **Cut**, **Copy** and **Paste**. You will also find them on the short menu that opens when you right-click on a selected object. These are used for copying and moving data within and between applications.

- **Copy** copies a selected block of text, picture, file or other object into a special part of memory called the *Clipboard*.

- **Cut** deletes selected data from the original application, but places a copy into the Clipboard.

- **Paste** copies the data from the Clipboard into a different place in the same application, or into a different application – as long as this can handle data in that format.

The data normally remains in the Clipboard until new data is copied or cut into it, or until Windows is shut down. (Some applications have a **Clear Clipboard** command.) If you want to see what's in the Clipboard – just for interest, as this serves few practical purposes – you can use the Clipboard Viewer. It should be on the **Programs ➡ Accessories ➡ Systems Tools** menu. (This is an optional utility and may not have been installed.)

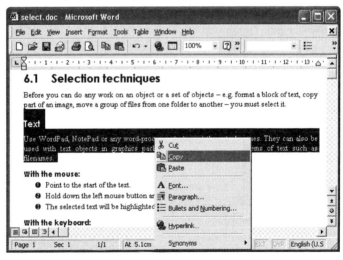

Figure 6.3 The short menu offers the quickest route to the Cut and Paste commands. If the Clipboard is empty, Paste will be 'greyed out' or omitted from the menu.

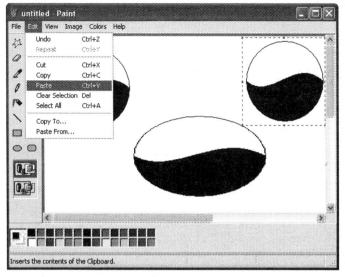

Figure 6.4 Pasting a copied image in Paint. Selected graphics usually have an enclosing frame with 'handles' at the corners and mid-sides. You can drag within the frame to move the object, or on the handles to resize it.

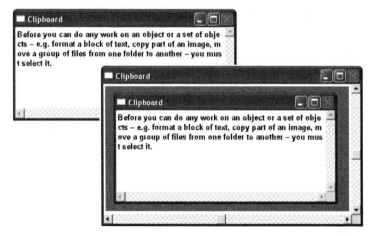

Figure 6.5 Two shots of the Clipboard Viewer. The first is after copying some text; the second is after capturing the screenshot of the Viewer – which is stored in the Clipboard! The Clipboard can hold data in any format, and the Viewer can display all major Windows formats.

6.3 Drag and drop

This is an alternative to Cut and Paste for moving objects within an application or between compatible applications. It is also the simplest way to rearrange files and folders, as you will see in the next chapter.

The technique is simple to explain:

1 Select the block of text or the object(s).

2 Point anywhere within the highlighted text or in the frame enclosing other objects.

3 Hold down the mouse button and drag the object across the screen or, with text, move the cursor (which is now ▯).

4 Release the button to drop the object into its new position.

In practice, accurate positioning depends upon good mouse control. And one of the best ways to improve your mouse control is to play the games. The card games use drag-and-drop for moving cards; Minesweeper helps to build speed and accuracy. (Remember this when you need an excuse.)

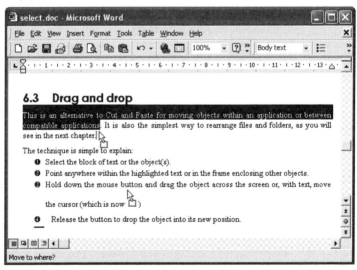

Figure 6.6 Dragging text in a word-processor. The target position for the text is marked by the thin bar to the left of the arrow.

Figure 6.7 You can drag a document from My Computer or Windows Explorer and drop it into a suitable application – this is sometimes quicker than opening files from within the application.

6.4 Scraps

A 'scrap' is a special sort of file parked on the Desktop. It is typically a fragment of a word-processor document – though it could be the whole of one. Scraps can be used as highly visible reminders of urgent jobs, or to hold blocks of text that you will reuse in other files, or simply as temporary storage.

What distinguishes a scrap from an ordinary file are the ways that it is created and used.

1 Set the word-processor window into Restore mode so that some of the Desktop is visible.

2 Select the text.

3 Drag the selection and drop it on the Desktop.

4 To reuse the scrap, either drag it into the application window,

Or

5 Double-click on it to open the application and load in the scrap document.

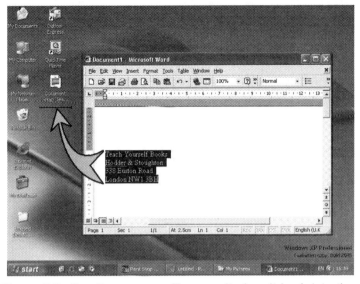

Figure 6.8 Creating a scrap. To reuse it, drag it back into the application.

Summary

- Text can be selected with the mouse or the keyboard.

- Graphics and other objects are selected by dragging an outline around them, or by using the mouse in conjunction with Shift or Ctrl.

- Selected data can be cut or copied to the Clipboard, then pasted into the same or a different application.

- Use the Clipboard Viewer to see what's in the Clipboard.

- Text and some objects can be moved by drag and drop.

- Text can be stored on the Desktop as scraps.

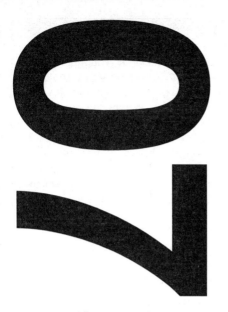

07

files and folders

In this chapter you will learn

- about My Computer and Windows Explorer
- how to manage folders
- about move and copy files
- how to recover files from the Recycle Bin
- how to find lost files

Aims of this chapter

To be able to use your computer efficiently, you must know how to manage your files – how to find, copy, move, rename and delete them – and how to organize the folders on your disks. In Windows XP, these jobs can be done through either Windows Explorer or My Computer – the two are almost identical. In this chapter we will have a look at these and see how they can be used for file and folder management. We will also look at creating links between documents and applications, and at the Recycle Bin – a neat device which makes it much less likely that you will delete files by accident.

7.1 Disks and folders

A floppy disk holds 1.4 Mb of data – enough for a few decent-sized documents. A typical hard drive can hold 20 Gigabytes – over 12,000 times as much! Obviously, with this much storage space, it must be organized if you are ever to find anything. The organization comes through *folders*.

A folder is an elastic-sided division of the disk. It can contain any number of files and subfolders – which can contain other subfolders, and so on *ad infinitum*. The structure is sometimes described as a tree. The *root* is at the drive level. The main folders branch off from here, and each may have a complex set of branches leading from it.

At the simplest, a C: drive might contain three folders – *My Documents*, *Program Files* (with subfolders for each application) and *Windows* (which has subfolders for the sets of programs and files that make up the Windows system). You can create new folders, rename, delete or move them to produce your own structure.

Floppy folders

You can also create folders on a floppy disk, if you want to keep several distinct sets of files on one disk.

7.2 My Computer/Windows Explorer

My Computer and Windows Explorer are two ways of using the same program – and though it may not seem it at first, Internet Explorer is yet another aspect of the same thing. They look a little different – at least in their default settings – and have slightly different selections of tools, but are otherwise the same.

The simple proof of this is that you can change any one into the other. Click on an Internet link or type an Internet address into My Computer or Windows Explorer and it will become Internet Explorer. Start to browse your hard disk from Internet Explorer and it will become Windows Explorer.

My Computer can only be started from the Desktop icon. It is Windows Explorer at its simplest, with the display set to do no more than show the contents of one drive or folder. It is convenient if you just want to work in one folder.

If you set My Computer so that it opens a new window for every folder (one of the *Folder Options*, see page 93), it can also be used for reorganizing your file storage.

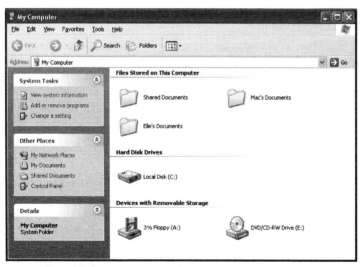

Figure 7.1 My Computer, shown here as it first appears.

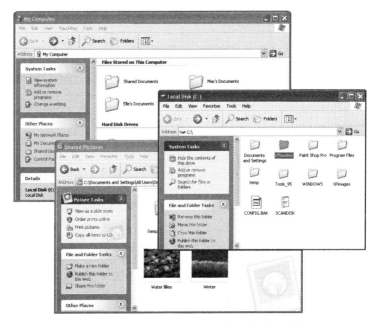

Figure 7.2 Run My Computer in multiple windows if you want to move files between the folders.

Common Tasks

When My Computer first opens, the panel on the left of the window displays *common tasks*. The selection varies, depending upon where you are in the system and what sort of file, if any, is selected at the time.

There will always be a set labelled **Other Places**, offering quick links to key parts of the system; and a **Details** box, telling you more about the currently selected folder or file – and if it is an image, showing a preview.

The **File or Folder Tasks** set will normally be present. There are some important commands here, which we shall be looking at shortly.

If you are at the top of the C:\ drive, the **System Tasks** set will be present, while if you are in a picture folder, the **Picture Tasks** set will be there, offering simple ways to view, print or copy pictures.

If you are running My Computer in a fairly small window, you may not be able to see all of the Tasks at once. Use the scroll bar to travel up and down through the sets, or click the double chevron icon in the top right to shrink the display down to the heading – click again to show the tasks.

Folders

As an alternative to the *Common Tasks*, you can have a Folders display in the left-hand panel (the **Explorer Bar**). Click the **Folders** button in the toolbar to switch to this. (And if you have used earlier versions of Windows, you will see that My Computer has been changed into Windows Explorer.) This style of display gives you easier ways to switch between folders, and to move files between them. If you find that you prefer to work in this mode, you can open Windows Explorer directly from the **Accessories** menu.

The **Folders** display shows the disk drives, folders and network connections in a branching structure. A ⊞ icon to the left of a folder name shows that the folder has subfolders. Click this to open up the branch. The icon changes to ⊟ and clicking this will close the branch.

When a folder is selected 🗁, its files and subfolders are listed in the main pane. Files can be listed by name, type, date or size, and displayed as thumbnails or icons, with or without details (see section 7.4).

If it has been turned on (ticked in the **View** menu), the **Status bar** at the bottom shows the number of objects in the folder and the amount of memory they use, or the size of a selected file.

The controls

These are at the top of the window. The **Menu bar** is always visible. As with any Windows application, the full command set can be reached through the menu system, but those that you will use most often can be accessed faster through toolbar buttons or keyboard shortcuts.

Root   Top-level folders   Click for the Folders display

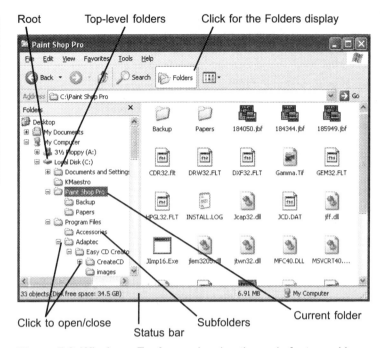

Click to open/close   Subfolders   Current folder
                      Status bar

Figure 7.3 Windows Explorer, showing the main features. Yours may well look different from this as there are many combinations of display options.

The available menu options vary when a file, folder or drive is selected.

There are three toolbars, all of which are optional – turn them on or off via the **View** menu.

The **Standard toolbar** (Figure 7.5) contains buttons for all essential jobs.

The **Address Bar** shows the current folder, and can be useful for moving around the system.

Links are shortcuts to places on the Internet (see Chapter 10).

Turn on the Status Bar?

Unlock the toolbars if you want to move them

Toolbars can be moved – drag the dotted handle up or down to move it, left or right to resize it

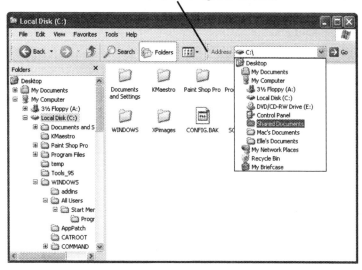

Figure 7.4 The **Address Bar** offers a quick way to get around – useful if you have opened up several levels of branches, producing a very long Folders display.

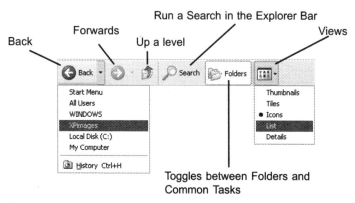

Run a Search in the Explorer Bar

Forwards

Back

Up a level

Views

Toggles between Folders and Common Tasks

Figure 7.5 The **Standard toolbar**. Drop-down lists from the Back and Forwards buttons provide an easy way to move between folders that you have selected earlier in the same session.

The Standard buttons

(with **menu commands**)

- *Back* (**View ➡ Go To ➡ Back**) and *Forward* (**View ➡ Go To ➡ Forward**) When you select a folder, it is added to their lists – you must go Back before you can go Forward.

- *Up* (**View ➡ Go To ➡ Up one level**) takes you up to the next level folder, or from a folder to the drive, or from a drive up to My Computer.

- *Search* opens the Search facility in the Explorer Bar.

- *Folders* toggles between displaying the folder list and the Common Tasks in the Explorer Bar.

- *Views* – leads to a drop-down list containing the main options from the View menu.

7.3 View options

Explorer Bar

If you click on **View** to open the menu, point to **Explorer Bar** and wait, this submenu opens.

Search helps you to find files and folders on your PC. Internet searches can also be run from here. This is the same Search as the one on the Start menu. We'll come back to it in section 7.11.

Favorites open up your list of favourite places – normally Web sites. We'll deal with this when we look at Internet Explorer.

Media provides tools for playing music and videos on your PC and for finding more media or listening to the Internet radio (Chapters 10 and 14).

History stores links to the sites and folders that you have visited recently – this is also more important in Internet Explorer, so we'll leave this until Chapter 10.

Folders is the default, displaying the folder structure.

Obviously, only one of these can occupy the Explorer Bar at any one time.

The **Tip of the Day** opens a new pane at the bottom right of the window and displays a helpful hint. You may find this useful when you first start.

Discuss links to online discussion servers, if you belong to one.

Pause over a filename and a panel
will pop up to show its details

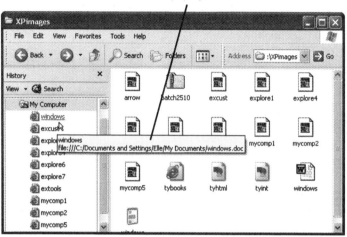

Figure 7.6 The **Explorer Bar** being used to display History – this can be the easiest way to find files that you have worked on recently.

7.4 Displaying and sorting files

Files and folders can be shown as a **Filmstrip** (if the folder holds pictures), **Thumbnails**, **Tiles**, **Icons**, **List** or **Details** – make your choice from the **View** menu or from the drop-down list on the **View** button.

Filmstrip shows thumbnails of the pictures, with a larger preview of the selected picture above.

Thumbnails shows – if possible – a miniature image of each file. It is, of course, best for use with images, but it can be handy for Web pages and some formatted documents.

Figure 7.7 The **Filmstrip View** is a good way to browse through a folder of pictures – it works much better on a bigger window!

Figure 7.8 The **Thumbnails View** is excellent for finding images and some types of formatted files – but you don't get many to a screenful.

Figure 7.9 The **Tiles View** has easy-to-see icons and tells you the key details about each file.

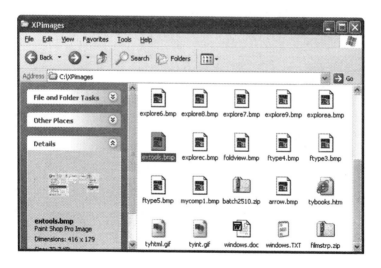

Figure 7.10 The **Icons View** displays a lot of files onto the screen – List View packs even more on – but you can see the details of any chosen file if you have Common Tasks in the Explorer Bar.

Tiles displays for each file a large icon (so it is easy to identify the type), plus details of its type, size, date and author (if appropriate).

Icons and **List** differ mainly in the size of the icons and in the order – icons has slightly larger images and lists across the screen. Both are good for selecting sets of files (see page 102).

Details gives a column display under the headings Name, Size, Type and Modified. Click on a heading to sort the files in ascending order by that feature. Click a second time to sort them in descending order. This display is useful for tracking down files that you were working on at a certain date (but have forgotten the names), or for finding old or large files if you need to create some space.

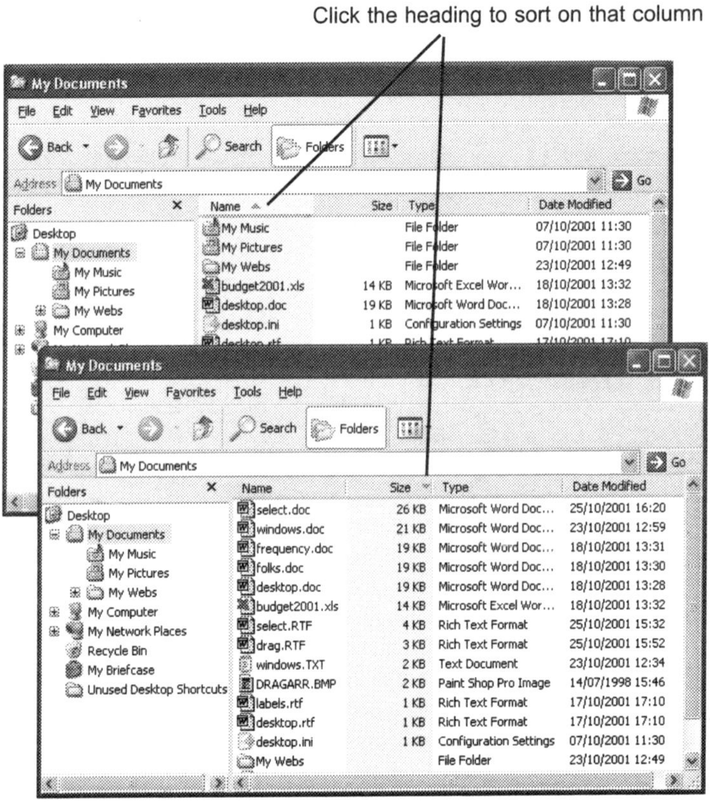

Click the heading to sort on that column

Figure 7.11 The **Details** display allows you to sort the files easily.

Arrange Icons

The **View** ➡ **Arrange Icons By** menu command can be used to sort the files by **Name**, **Type**, **Size** or **Date** in any mode, whether or not the details are displayed on screen. If you are in Details View to start with, there is also a **View** ➡ **Arrange Icons By** ➡ **Show in Groups** option that will group the files on the currently selected column header. This can be a neat way to get your files together before you start to copy, move, backup or otherwise organize them.

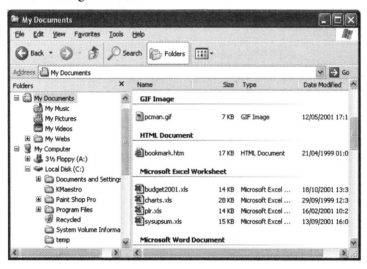

Figure 7.12 The **Details View** with files arranged into groups.

7.5 Folder Options

The **Folder Options** are crucial to how you view and manage your files and folders. To reach it, open the **Tools** menu and select **Folder Options**.

On the **General** tab under **Tasks**, select **Show common tasks in folders** if you want a 'richer' experience, with fancier folders and automatic previews of files. **Use Windows classic folders** for a simpler file display.

In the **Browse Folders** option, opening each folder in its own window is useful for moving files from one to another, but can produce a cluttered screen. When you actually open a folder,

Figure 7.13
The **General** tab of
Folder Options.

you can switch to the opposite by holding down [**Control**]. If you have selected **Open each folder in the same window**, hold down [**Control**] when opening to have the folder open in a new window.

Note: the **Click items as follows** option applies to all files and folders, whether on the Desktop or in My Computer/Windows Explorer.

View options

Some of the options here really are just fine-tuning, and you can come back and play with these when you want to see what they do. The more significant ones are covered here.

Most of the **Advanced Settings** should be left at their defaults until you have been using Windows for a while. A couple are worth checking now.

Hidden files – Windows XP 'hides' essential files, to prevent accidental deletion. They can be shown if you want to see them, or these and system files – also crucial – can be hidden. For safety, hide them.

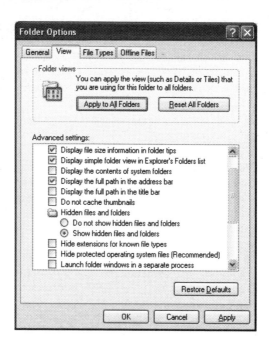

Figure 7.14
The **View** tab of
Folder Options.

The option **Remember each folder's view settings** will retain the separate settings from one session to the next. These can be different for each folder – which makes sense. You may well want more detail in folders that contain documents than in those that contain program or system files.

Click **Apply to All Folders** if you want the current settings – principally the choice of **View** – to be applied to all folders. If you have got into a bit of a mess with your options (easily done!), click **Reset All Folders** to go back to the original settings.

7.6 File Types

Documents can be associated with applications, so that picking a document from the **My Recent Documents** list on the **Start** menu or out of a folder will start up its application and open the document within it.

The **File Types** tab of **Folder Options** lists all the 'registered' file types – the ones associated with applications. There should be lots there already as Windows sets up associations between a whole host of documents and applications when it first starts, and most applications will add their own types to the list as they are installed. Select any one of them from the list, and in the bottom part of the panel you will see the details for the extension(s) that mark this type and the application that the document opens with.

New File Types

Not all applications come equipped with the installation routines to set up associations for you – older software, and shareware downloaded from the Internet may not make the links. If you want to be really thorough about it, you can go through all your applications, making a note of the file types that they can handle, then go through the File Types list and check that all are included. If any have been overlooked, you can create the association here, by clicking the **New** button. It's not a particularly difficult process – but it takes time, and there is an easier way to do things.

Figure 7.15 The **File Types** tab – scroll through the list. You will be amazed at how many types your system knows about already!

1 Close the **Folder Options** panel and forget about file types for now.

2 When, at some point in the future, you try to open a document of an unregistered type, you will be presented with the **Open With** panel.

3 Scroll through the list of applications and select the right one for the type. If you cannot see it in the list, but know that it is on your system, click the **Browse...** button and track down the .exe program file.

4 If you want to give a description (to appear in the **File Types** list), do so, but this is not essential.

5 Click **OK**.

• Now try to open the document and the associated application should run.

If you do not want to set up a permanent link with an application, clear this box and the document will be opened with the chosen program on this occasion only.

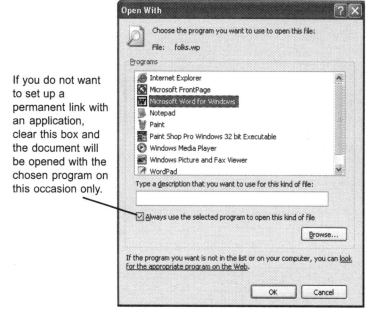

Figure 7.16 The **Open With** dialog box – use this to set up an association between a new file type and an application.

7.7 Organizing folders

Windows XP sets up one folder for your files, called *My Documents*. This is unlikely to be enough for very long. You may need to create folders if:

- you will be storing more than a few dozen documents – it's hard to find stuff in crowded folders;

- more than one person uses the PC – if they have user accounts (section 8.7), they will each have their own *My Documents* area, but extra organized space is often needed;

- your documents fall into distinct categories – personal, hobbies, different areas of work, etc.

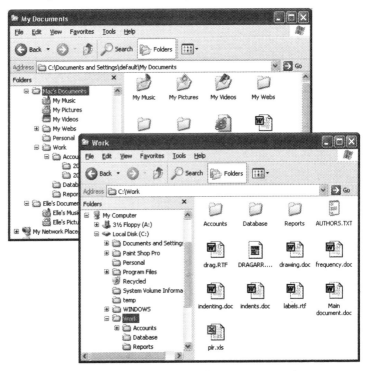

Figure 7.17 Two approaches to a folder structure for someone who uses the PC for work and personal use. In the top one, the new folders have been created with the user's Documents folder; in the lower, the folders are all at the main level. Either works just as well.

Mixed contents

Putting documents of different types in one folder is not as confusing as it might seem. It might look untidy when you view it through My Computer – though sorting by Type will help to clarify. In practice, you mainly access your documents through applications, and when you open a file there, the **Open File** dialog boxes will normally only list those of the right type.

Creating folders

A new folder can be created at any time, and at any point in the folder structure. Here's how:

1 In Explorer, select the folder which will contain the new one, or select the drive letter for a new top-level folder.

2 Open the **File** menu, point to **New** then select **Folder**.

3 Replace *New Folder* with a meaningful name.

♦ If you decide the folder is in the wrong place, select it and drag it into place in the All Folders list.

Select the containing folder   Use File ➡ New ➡ Folder

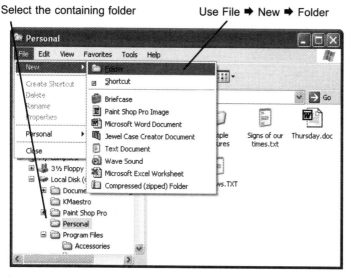

Figure 7.18 Select the containing folder before creating a folder.

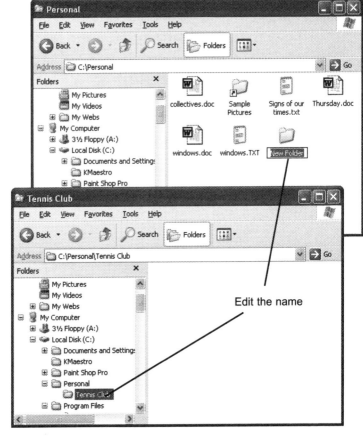

Figure 7.19 The new folder will need renaming.

Folders are files

We think of folders as containers, but to the PC they are files, with lists of the names and disk locations of other files. They are special – you cannot read them, and the system interprets them to create the folder displays – but they can be renamed, copied and deleted just the same as document files.

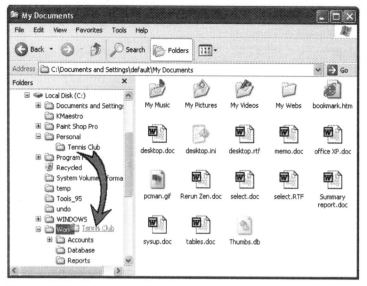

Figure 7.20 Folders can be dragged to rearrange the structure.

7.8 Creating shortcuts

A Desktop shortcut offers the simplest and quickest way to start an application or open a folder – as long as you can see the Desktop! You can create new shortcuts in several ways. This is probably the easiest.

Application shortcuts

1 Open the application's folder in Explorer or My Computer.

2 Locate the program file. If you are not sure whether it is the right one, click (or double-click) on it. If the application runs, it's the right file.

3 Drag the file onto the Desktop.

4 Edit the name to remove 'Shortcut to...', if you like. •

Shortcuts to folders

1 Select the folder in Explorer or My Computer.

2 Hold the right mouse button down and drag the icon onto the Desktop.

3 Select **Create Shortcut(s) Here**.

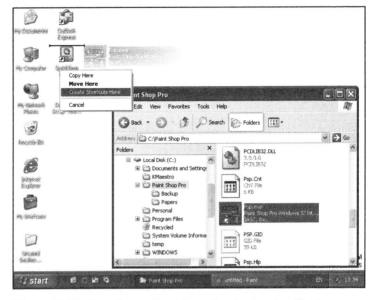

Figure 7.21 Creating a **Desktop shortcut** using Explorer.

7.9 File management

As a general rule, application files – the ones that make up the software – should be left well alone. Start messing with these and your programs may well not work. Document files are a different matter. They need to be managed actively or your folders will become cluttered, making it hard to find files.

Selecting files

Before you can do anything with files, you must select them.

• *To select a single file*, point to it (if you use the Web Page mode), or click once on it (in Classic mode).

• *To select a set of adjacent files*, click on the window to the right of the top one and drag an outline over the set;

Or

• Select the first, hold down the **Shift** key, and select the last.

• *To select scattered files*, select the first, hold down the **Control** key and select the rest in turn.

Drag an outline or hold down **Shift** to select a set

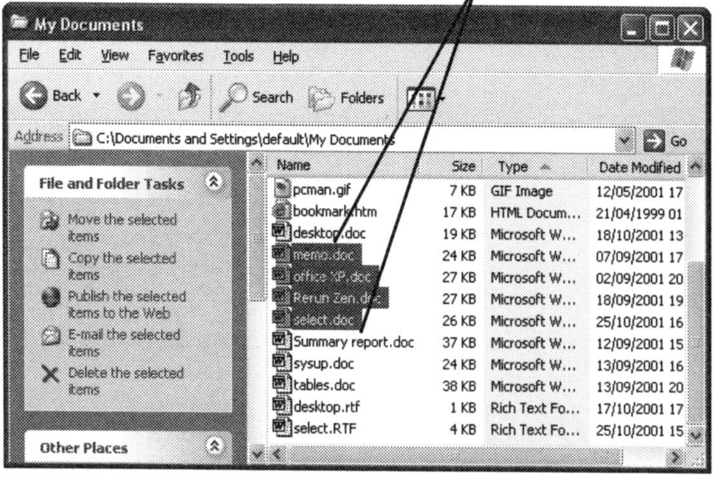

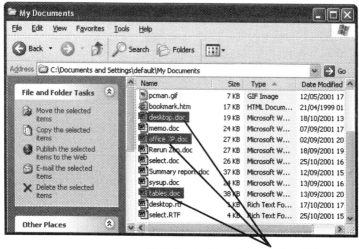

Figure 7.22 Adjacent files can be selected as a block.

Hold **Control** to select scattered files

Figure 7.23 Scattered files can also be selected together – it's
fiddly, but still simpler than repeating operations on individual files.

Moving and copying files

Files are easily moved or copied. The technique is similar for both.

1   Select the file(s).

2   Scroll through the **All Folders** display and/or open subfolders, if necessary, until you can see the target folder.

3   Drag the file(s) across the screen and over the target folder to highlight it, then drop the file(s) there.

◆   If the original and target folders are both on the same disk, this will move the selected file(s).

◆   If the folders are on different disks, or your target is a floppy disk, this will copy the file(s).

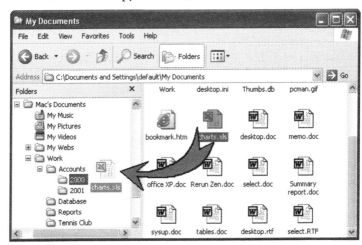

Figure 7.24 If you can see the target folder, you can drag files into it.

If you want to move a file from one disk to another, or copy within the same disk, hold down the right mouse button while you drag. When you release the button, select **Move** or **Copy** from the short menu.

Dragging is simplest in Explorer. If you are using My Computer, you can open multiple windows and drag across the screen between them.

Copy To Folder and Move To Folder

If your mouse control is a bit iffy, things can go astray when dragging files and folders. A slower, but more reliable alternative is to use the **Copy To Folder** and **Move To Folder** commands.

1 Select the file(s).

2 To move a file, use **Move this file** in the Common Tasks or the **Edit ➧ Move to Folder...** command.

Or

3 To copy, use **Copy this file** in the Common Tasks or **Edit ➧ Copy to Folder...**

4 The **Move/Copy Items** dialog box will open. Work your way down through the folder structure and select the target folder, then click **OK**.

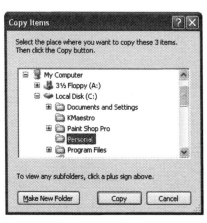

◆ If you copy a file into the same folder, it will be renamed '*Copy of...*' (the original filename).

105

files and folders

07

Renaming files

If you want to edit or retype a file's name, select the file and press **F2** on your keyboard, or use **Rename** from the **File** or shortcut menu. Change the name as required and press **Enter** to fix the new name.

◆ If you are working in Classic mode (where you click to select), a second click on the filename will switch into edit mode.

Extensions

When renaming files, do not change their extensions! If you do, you will lose the document–application link (page 95).

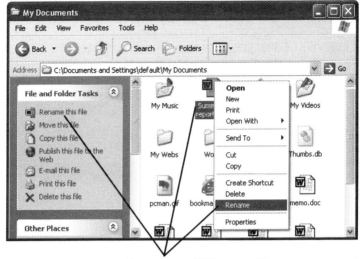

Figure 7.25 Select the file and press [F2] or use a Rename command.

Sending files elsewhere

The **Send To** command on the **File** or shortcut menus offers a simple way to copy a file to a floppy disk or to your Mail system for sending by e-mail.

Just select the destination to begin.

Deleting files

If a file is no longer needed, select it and press **Delete** on your keyboard or use the **File ➔ Delete** command. If you delete a folder, all its files are also deleted.

Windows XP makes it very difficult to delete files by accident! First, you have to confirm – or cancel – the deletion at the prompt. Second, nothing is permanently deleted at this stage. Instead, the file or folder is transferred to the Recycle Bin. Let's have a look at that now.

7.10 The Recycle Bin

The true value of the Recycle Bin is only fully appreci- ated by those of us who have used systems which lack this refinement, and have spent hours – or sometimes days – replacing files deleted in error! In practice, you will rarely need the Bin, but when you do, you will be glad that it is there!

If you find that you need a deleted file, it can be restored easily.

1 Open the Recycle Bin, from the Desktop icon or from My Computer (at the end of the Folders list).

2 Select the file.

3 Open the **File** menu, or right-click for the shortcut menu and select **Restore**.

◆ If the file's folder has also been deleted, it will be re-created first, so that the file can go back where it came from.

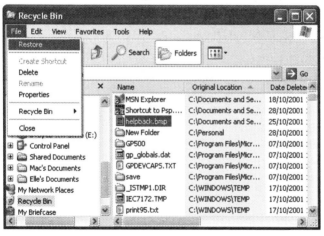

Figure 7.26 Files deleted in error can be restored from the Bin.

One of the main reasons for deleting files is to free up disk space, but as long as they are in the Recycle Bin, they are still on the disk. So, make a habit of emptying the bin from time to time. There is an **Empty...** option on the Bin's right-click menu (in the Folder list), but this should only be used when you are absolutely sure that there is nothing in it that you might want to restore.

- Play safe! Open the Bin, check its contents carefully and restore any files you deleted accidentally, before using the **File ➡ Empty Recycle Bin** command.

- The default settings allows the Recycle Bin to use up to 10% of the drive's capacity, which should work well. If you want to change this, right-click on the Bin's icon to open its Properties panel and set the level there.

7.11 Search

Windows XP has several Search utilities, but the one we are interested in here is **File or Folders**, which can track down lost files for you, hunting for them by name, location, contents, date, type and/or size. If you organize your folders properly, and always store files in the right places, you'll never need this utility. However, if you are like me, you will appreciate it.

- In Explorer, click the **Search** icon .
Or

- Click **Start**, point to **Search** and select **For Files or Folders**.

A simple search can be by all or part of the filename or for some text within a file – or a combination of the two. At the simplest, you may remember what the file was called, but not where you stored it. Just type in all or part of the name and click **Search**. Within a few seconds the missing file should be listed on the right of the window – and it may well be accompanied by other files, especially if you gave only part of the name. Double-click on the file to open it, or make a note of its folder so that you can find it easily again later.

It's just as easy to set up a search where you can remember some significant words within the text. Type in the word or phrase and click **Search**. This time the search will take a little longer as the system will search through the text of files, rather than simply checking their filenames.

Suppose, for example, you were looking for a letter to Mr Ree but could not remember what you called it or where you stored it. You at least know that it contained his name and that it was a Word document – and so would have the .doc extension. You could simply give 'Mr Ree' as the phrase, and the search would find it, but if you also gave 'doc' in the filename slot, it would speed things up, as the search would then only have to read through document files (plus any others that happened to have 'doc' somewhere in their names) and could ignore all the rest.

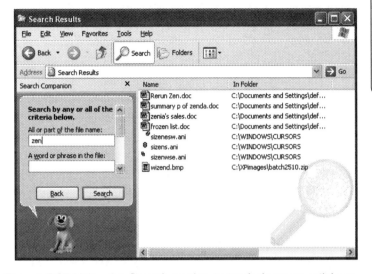

Figure 7.27 Using the **Search** routine to track down an article on Zen. If you want to change or turn off the animated character, right-click on it to reach the options.

If you look further down the search panel you will find a number of ways in which to focus a search. The first is to specify which drives or folders to start looking in – this will speed up the search. Note that the search will normally look into all the subfolders below the start point, which is, of course, what you would normally want it to do.

The **When was it modified?** options are useful if you know when a file was created, modified or last accessed. You can look for files within the last week, month or year, or set specific date limits – and the drop-down calendars provide a very neat way to set dates!

A **What size is it?** setting by itself will rarely help you to find a file, but in combination with other features might prove useful – if nothing else, it will rule out files of the wrong size.

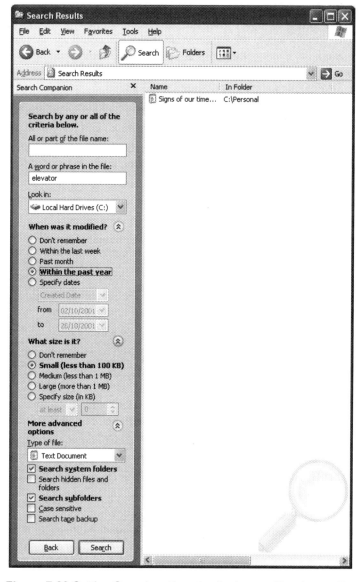

Figure 7.28 Setting Search options to pin down a file – in practice you would rarely use more than one or two of these at a time. (I've turned off the Assistant to save screen space!)

In the **More advanced options,** the most useful is probably the *Type of file* – select the type from the (long!!) drop-down list. The others are for more specialized use.

Summary

♦ Folders on hard (and floppy) disks create organized storage for your files.

♦ My Computer and Windows Explorer are two views of the same program. This is the main utility for managing files and folders, and has a comprehensive set of tools.

♦ The View and Folder options allow you to set up the display to suit yourself.

♦ The simplest way to create a new File Types association is to select the appropriate application when Windows asks you what it should open a document with.

♦ Files can be displayed in various views and can be sorted into name, size, type or date order.

♦ You should create folders for each area of your computer work. Folders can be created within other folders if needed.

♦ Desktop shortcuts can be created by dragging file or folder icons from Explorer or My Computer onto the Desktop.

♦ Files can be moved, copied, renamed or deleted.

♦ To select sets of files, drag an outline with the mouse, or use the mouse in combination with Shift or Ctrl.

♦ When renaming files, do not change the extensions, as these identify the type of document.

♦ The Send command offers a simple way to copy a file to a floppy disk, or to e-mail it to someone.

♦ When a file is deleted, it is transferred to the Recycle Bin. If necessary, files can be restored from the Bin.

♦ The Search routine allows you to track down files through their name (or part of it!), location, date, type or size.

08

the control panel

In this chapter you will learn

- about customizing your system
- how to add or remove fonts, programs and Windows components
- how to adjust the mouse and keyboard
- about user accounts
- how to make your system more accessible

Aims of this chapter

Windows' plug and play facility for new hardware, and the installation routines for new software, help to ensure that your system is properly configured. However, there are some things which Windows cannot do for you as they depend upon your preferences. The Control Panel is where you find the tools to customize your setup to suit yourself. In this chapter we will be looking at eight of the key components. Even if you are happy with the way that your system is running – or if you are hesitant about making changes that you might regret – do have a look at these. All the dialog boxes have a **Cancel** button!

8.1 Using the Panel

To open the Control Panel, click the **Start** button then click its link in the middle of the right-hand side.

The panel has two alternative displays:

◆ **Category View** (Figure 8.1) is the default and probably the best view for new users. It groups the components by function and guides you through the tasks.

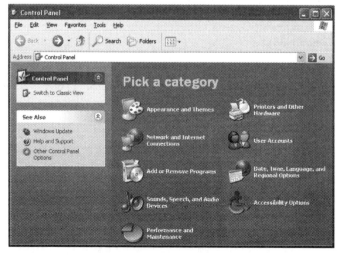

Figure 8.1 The **Control Panel** in Category View.

+ **Classic View** (Figure 8.2) will be familiar to users of previous versions of Windows. It takes you directly to the components, and for the most part – though not always – it is obvious which you should use to customize which part of your PC.

We'll work through the Category View.

Figure 8.2 The **Control Panel** in Classic View – use this for quicker access direct to the components.

See Also

Not all of the categories are covered in this chapter, as some are dealt with in other contexts, elsewhere in the book.

For the **Display** aspects of **Appearance and Themes**, see Chapter 2; for the **Taskbar and Start menu**, see Chapter 9; Folder Options were covered in section 7.5.

For **Network and Internet Connections**, see sections 14.3, *Home Networking*, and 10.4, *Internet Options*.

For **Performance and Maintenance**, see Chapter 12, *Maintaining your system*.

For **Printers**, see Chapter 13; **Other Hardware** – specifically, the mouse and the keyboard, are dealt with here.

8.2 Appearance and Themes – fonts

You will not need this facility very often, but it's as well to know how to find it. The Fonts folder can be reached from the **See Also** links in the Appearance and Themes part of the Control Panel.

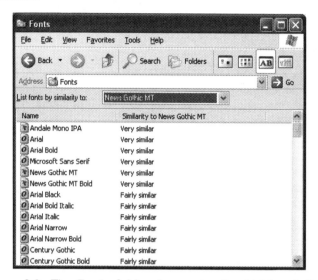

Figure 8.3 The **Fonts folder**, here using the *List by similarity* view. Choose a font from the drop-down list, and the whole set is then listed in order of closeness of match. Some fonts have Bold, Italic and Bold Italic variations. Within a word-processor you will normally only see the main name in the font list – the Bold or Italic versions are then used if these effects are selected later. This view is useful for weeding out excess fonts – to remove an unwanted font, select it then use **Delete** on the **File** menu.

A font is a typeface design, identified by a name. Within one font you will get type in a range of sizes (some are more variable than others), and the appearance may be varied by the use of bold, italic or other styles.

Fonts can be divided into three categories:

◆ **Serif** – like this (Times New Roman), marked by little tails at the ends of strokes. The tails (serifs) make the text easier to read, which is why serif fonts are normally chosen for large blocks of text.

- **Sans serif** – like this (Arial), with simpler lines. Sans fonts are typically used for headings and captions.
- **Display** – *decorative* fonts *of all kinds*. These are mainly used for headlines, posters, adverts, party invitations and special effects.

There are thousands of fonts in the world, and a couple of dozen of the best of these are supplied with Windows XP. You will get more with any word-processor that you install, and you can buy CDs full of fonts.

You do not need a huge number. Professional designers normally work to the 'three-font' rule: no more than three fonts on any one page – one serif, one sans serif and one display – using different sizes and styles for variety and emphasis.

The three fonts that you use may well be different for each project, but three or four serif and sans fonts and a dozen or so display fonts should be enough for most purposes. The more you have, the longer it will take to scroll through the font list whenever you are formatting text!

Do include Times New Roman and Arial in your selection. These two are used far more often than any others, simply because they are clear, attractive and highly readable. They are also – along with `Courier New` – the standard fonts for Web pages.

Viewing fonts

If you want to see what a font looks like, just click on it. A viewer will open, showing samples of the characters in a range of sizes. If the font is to be used for extensive work, and it is especially important that it looks just right, click the **Print** button to get a printed copy – there are often subtle differences between the screen display and printed output.

Click **Done** or ⊠ to close the viewer, or select another font – a second copy of the viewer will open – if you want to compare them side by side.

Figure 8.4 The font viewer in use. True Type fonts are virtually identical on screen and paper. If they are not True Type, they are more likely to vary. In any case, a test print is often worth doing.

Installing fonts

If you have bought fonts on disk or CD-ROM, or have downloaded them from the Internet, they must be installed properly before they can be used.

1 Open the **File** menu and select **Install New Font**.

2 At the **Add Fonts** panel, select the drive and folder.

3 Select the fonts from the list, pressing **Ctrl** while you click if you want to pick several.

4 If the font file is already on your hard disk, clear the **Copy fonts to Fonts folder** checkbox. There is no point in duplicating storage.

5 Click **OK**.

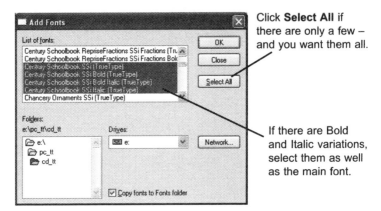

Click **Select All** if
there are only a few –
and you want them all.

If there are Bold
and Italic variations,
select them as well
as the main font.

8.3 Add/Remove Programs

Any software that is written to the Windows XP specifications
will be registered with the system when it is installed, so that it
can be uninstalled, or the installation adjusted later through
this panel.

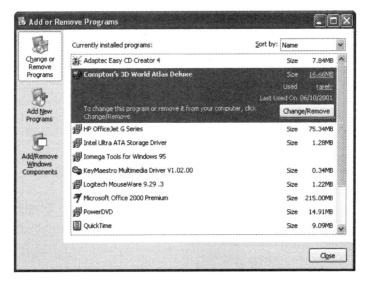

Figure 8.5 Software can be uninstalled, or its components varied
here. Click **Change/Remove** to go to a routine to uninstall a
program or to select components to add or remove from a suite

- New software can be installed through the **Add New Programs** tab, but you can do it equally well by running the 'install' or 'setup' program directly.

Change or Remove Programs

Use this facility to clear unwanted software off your system, or to add or remove components from suites, such as Microsoft Office. If you simply delete a program's folder in My Computer, it may remove all or most of the software's files – though there may be others scattered elsewhere in your disks – but it will not remove the entry in the Start menu, or the File Types associations. A proper uninstall will (normally) do a full clean-out from your system.

Windows Setup

Windows XP is a huge package with a vast set of utilities and accessories – most people will use only a limited number of these and no one will use all of them. You may decide, after having used Windows XP for a while, that some components are a waste of space – and then again, you may need to put them back later!

1 Find your Windows CD and switch to the **Windows Setup** panel.

   The components are listed, with a checkbox beside the name to indicate its status, and a disk space given on the right.

The checkboxes can be in one of three states:

   ☑ all components selected under this heading

   ☒ some components selected

   ☐ no components selected

2 Select a **Component** heading, e.g. Accessories and Utilities, and click the **Details** button – if the button is greyed out, the component has no options.

3 At the next panel, tick the checkbox to add a component, or clear it to remove an existing one. Some components at this level have subsets of options – the **Details** button will be active if they have. Click **OK** when you have finished.

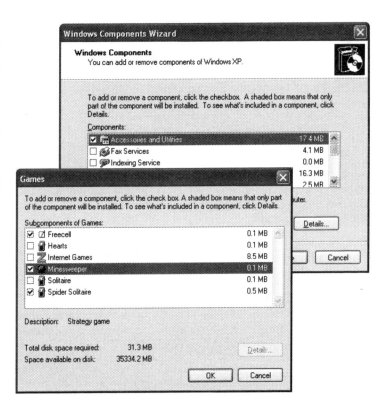

Figure 8.6 Adjusting the Windows Setup. As you select the components to add or remove, the panel displays the total space required. The full set of optional components takes around 45Mb.

4 Click **Next** on the main panel when you have done, and wait while Windows adds or removes components. You may have to restart the PC for some changes to take effect.

8.4 Sounds, Speech and Audio Devices

Windows can attach sounds to certain events so that you get, for example, a fanfare at start up and a warning noise when you are about to do something you may later regret. Some of these are just for fun, others can be very useful. If you watch the keyboard, rather than the screen, when you are typing, then

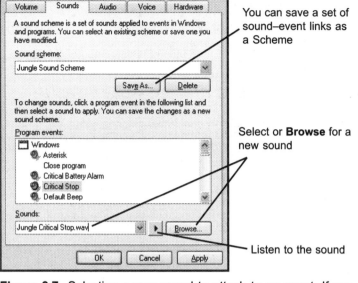

You can save a set of sound–event links as a Scheme

Select or **Browse** for a new sound

Listen to the sound

Figure 8.7 Selecting a new sound to attach to an event. If you want to turn off a sound, select None in the **Sounds** list.

an audible warning can help to alert you to a situation before it becomes a problem.

The **Change the sound scheme** link leads you to the **Sounds** tab of the **Sounds and Audio Devices Properties** panel, where you can decide which events are to be accompanied by a sound, and which sounds to use. There are several sound schemes and a selection of individual sounds supplied with Windows, or you can use your own .wav files. (You can create your own files with Sound Recorder – explore it one day, it's simple to use.)

1 If you want to change the overall nature of your sounds, first select a scheme from the list.

2 To change the sound assigned to an event, select the program event from the list then either pick a sound from the **Sounds** list, or click **Browse** and locate the file on your hard disk.

3 Click ▶ to hear the current sound.

4 When you have finished, click **Save As...** if you want to save the scheme so that it can be reapplied later.

While you have this Properties panel open, you might want to adjust the **Volume** (both the **Adjust the system volume** and **Change the speaker settings** links lead to this). The other options are best left at their defaults, as long as the audio is working properly. If you do experience problems, there is a **Test Hardware** button on the **Voice** tab, and a **Troubleshoot** button on the **Hardware** tab.

8.5 Mouse

Tuning the mouse to your hand is very important, so it's a bit surprising that the Properties box for this key component is tucked away on the **Printers and Other Hardware** section. You'll find the link in the **Pick a Control Panel** icon area.

Buttons

The first tab of the **Mouse Properties** panel is for the **Buttons**. If you are left-handed, you may be tempted by the option **Switch primary and secondary buttons** (so you would use the

When the double-click speed is set correctly, you should be able to open and close the folder effortlessly

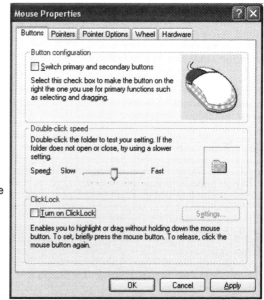

Figure 8.8 The **Buttons** tab of the **Mouse** panel.

one on the right for a simple click, and left-click to open context menus). Resist the tempation. It may make life easier when you first start to use your new PC, but you will be in a mess if you ever have to use anybody else's. Get used to the standard setting – it's not hard, I use my mouse with either hand.

The only crucial setting here is the **Double-click** speed. Test the current setting by double-clicking on the folder, and use the slider to adjust the response if necessary.

If you have trouble holding down a button while dragging, you might like to try turning on the **ClickLock** facility.

Pointers

The options here are almost entirely decorative, though obviously anything which makes it easier for you to see what you are doing must be beneficial. There are a dozen or so pointers, each related to a different mouse action. If you do not like some or all of the current set, select them one at a time and click **Browse**. You can then pick a new one from the pointers folder.

View the animated cursors in the Preview pane

If you don't like a pointer, select it and click Browse to find an alternative.

Figure 8.9 The **Pointers** tab of the **Mouse** panel.

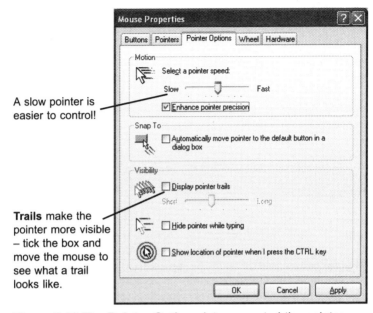

A slow pointer is easier to control!

Trails make the pointer more visible – tick the box and move the mouse to see what a trail looks like.

Figure 8.10 The **Pointer Options** let you control the pointer.

Motion

The **Pointer speed** controls how far and how fast the pointer moves in relation to mouse movements. To test this, move the mouse and watch the pointer. If you don't feel in control, set it slower. If it takes too long to get around the screen, set it faster. Click **Apply** and test again. Click **OK** when it feels right.

The **Pointer trail** option is only really relevant for laptop users. Pointers do not show up well on LCD screens, particularly when they are in motion. Turning on the trail makes them much easier to see.

8.6 Keyboard

The **Keyboard** panel is also in the **Printers and Other Hardware** section. How long your fingers linger on the keys affects the way that keystrokes are repeated. You normally want keystrokes to be picked up separately, but will sometimes want them to repeat – perhaps to create a line of ******.

I think I need to slow the repeat rate down a little further

Figure 8.11 Use the **Keyboard** panel to set the speed to suit you.

- The **Repeat delay** is how long to wait before starting to repeat – if you are heavy-fingered, set this to *Long*.

- The **Repeat rate** is how fast the characters are produced. This should match your reaction times.

Test the settings by typing in the test area, before you click **OK**.

8.7 User Accounts

Windows XP makes it easy for several people to share the use of one PC. Each user can have their own set of folders and their own customized Desktop and Start menu. To start work, users 'log on' by selecting their user name and entering a password (if set). Windows then loads their personalized settings for the Desktop and Start menu. When they start work, they have access to all the documents and programs on the shared area of the hard disk – normally most of it – and their own private folder, but not to other users' folders.

Here's how to set up an account for a new user.

1 Click the **User Accounts** link in the Control Panel.

2 Click **Create a new account**.

3 Enter the user's name and click **Next**.

4 Set the account type.

An *Administrator* has full access to the PC and can create and change user accounts and passwords.

A *Limited* user can only access his/her own files and anything in the Shared Documents folder.

In the home, you would probably set Administrator status for all users except those younger ones who might delete or change other people's files accidentally. If people use older Windows software, they may need to be Administrators as the progams may not run properly with Limited access.

5 Click **Create Account**.

The new user can later set, change or remove a password, change the picture or set up a .NET password – you'll need this if you want to join the Messenger service.

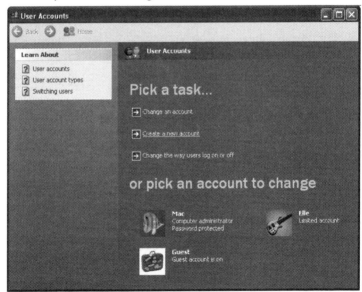

Figure 8.12 The **User Accounts** panel as seen by an administrator. From here an administrator can create new accounts, change the settings for an existing account or delete unwanted accounts.

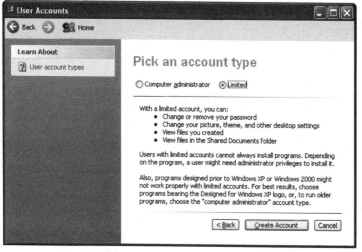

Figure 8.13 Users should only be set as *Limited* if essential for the security of other people's files.

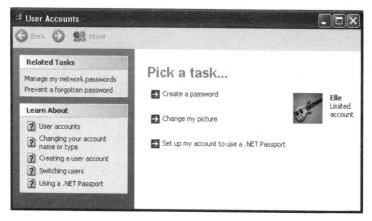

Figure 8.14 The **User Accounts** panel belonging to a Limited user. Passwords should only be created if needed – they can be a pain. If you do create one, click the **Prevent a forgotten password** link in the **Related Tasks** and create a 'password reset' disk. This will enable you to get back into the system should you later forget the password.

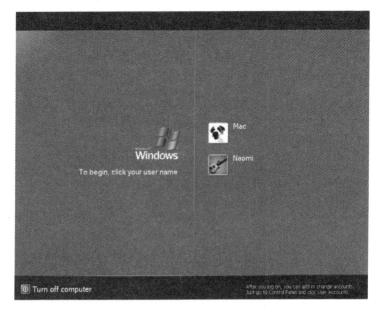

Figure 8.15 The startup screen for a PC with two users.

Figure 8.16 If a password is set, a password entry box appears when the user name is clicked. Passwords should only be set when they are essential, as they slow down logging on and forgetting them is a nuisance.

8.8 Date, Time, Language and Regional

Change the date and time

Even if you do not display the Clock on the Taskbar (see page 137), you should still make sure that the clock/calendar is correctly set if you want the date and time details to be right on your saved documents.

PCs are good time-keepers – Windows adjusts for Summer Time automatically – as long as they are set correctly at the start.

1 Go to the **Date, Time, Language and Regional Options** area and click on **Change the date and time**.

2 To change the date, select the month from the drop-down list and click on the day.

Select a Time Zone from the list

To set the time, select the digits and use the arrow buttons

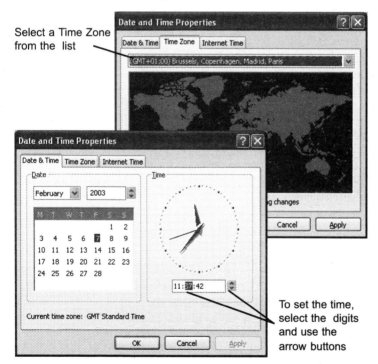

Figure 8.17 Setting the date and time.

3 To change the time, select the hour or minute figure and type the correct value, or use the little arrows to adjust the numbers.

4 If you need to change the time zone go to the **Time Zone** tab and select the zone from the drop-down list.

If you use the PC to connect to the Internet, you can keep your clock accurate by turning on the synchronization option on the Internet Time tab. The PC will then synchronize regularly with an Internet time server.

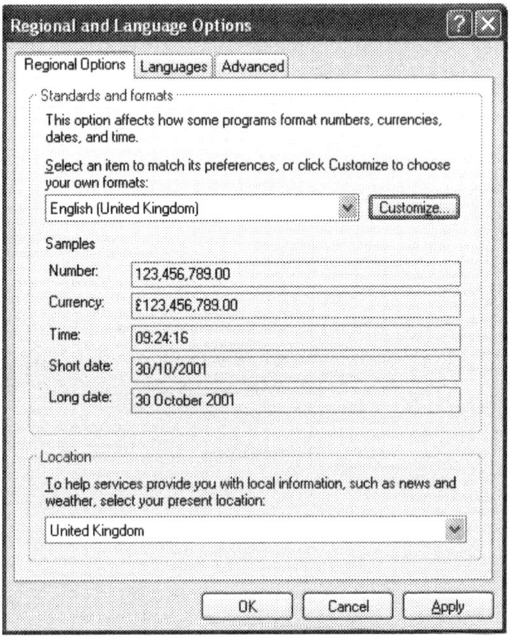

Figure 8.18
Setting the
regional options.

Change the format of numbers, dates and times

This option in the Date, Time, Language and Regional set leads to the **Regional and Language Options** panel. On the **Regional Options** tab you will see samples of the formats currently used for numbers, currency, time and dates. If you are happy to use the formats that are standard for your region, then all you need to do is select the country from the drop-down list. If you want to vary any of the settings, click **Customize** and define your formats as required.

Add other languages

Use this link if you want to be able to enter text using the keyboard for another language – and note that this is best suited to touch-typists who are used to a foreign keyboard. Most of us are better off selecting accented letters and the like from the Character Map (see page 227).

The link takes you to the **Languages** tab of the **Regional and Language Options** panel. Here's how to add a new language.

1 Click the **Details...** button.

2 At the **Text Services and Input Languages** dialog box, click **Add** then select the language.

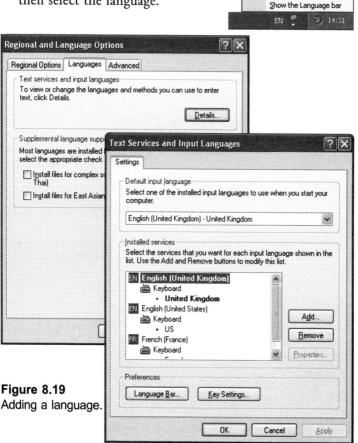

Figure 8.19
Adding a language.

◆ You can switch the keyboard using the Language bar on the right of the Taskbar. If you want to be able to switch using keyboard shortcuts, click on **Key Settings** and define the shortcuts.

8.9 Accessibility Options

The options here are designed to make life easier for people with disabilities, but are worth investigating by anyone who is less than comfortable with the keyboard or mouse.

Keyboard

StickyKeys allow you to get the **Shift, Ctrl** and **Alt** key combinations by pressing them in sequence rather than simultaneously.

FilterKeys control the point at which a keystroke is picked up, or is repeated, and the repeat rate. Most of these settings can also be controlled through the Keyboard component (page124).

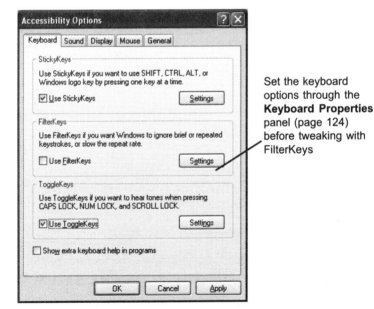

Set the keyboard options through the **Keyboard Properties** panel (page 124) before tweaking with FilterKeys

Figure 8.20 The **Keyboard** tab of the **Accessibility Options**.

If you still find that the keys are not responding as you would like after you have set the options there, come back and check out FilterKeys.

ToggleKeys will alert you when the Caps Lock, Num Lock or Scroll Lock keys are pressed. This is handy if, like me, you sometimes hit Caps Lock when aiming for Tab, and then type merrily on in CAPITALS!

All Settings panels have a **Keyboard shortcut** option. If used, the feature can be turned on and off – either to suit different users, or to suit the way you are working at that time.

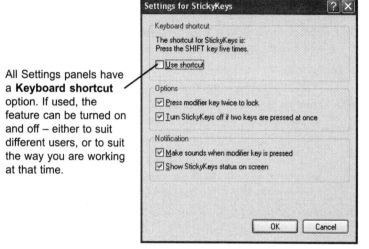

Figure 8.21 Almost all of the **Accessibility** options have **Settings** that can be configured to your needs.

Sound

The main option on this tab turns on visual clues to replace, or emphasize sound prompts.

Display

The high contrast display options, which are also available through the Display Properties panel (Chapter 2), can be turned on here.

Mouse

The **MouseKeys** option allows you to use the number pad keys to make mouse actions. The central key (5) does the left click; minus and 5 do the right-click; the number keys (7, 8, 9, 4, 6, 1, 2, 3) move the mouse.

General

If you have set up an accessibility option so that it can be toggled on and off as required, go to this tab to define when to turn options off, and how to notify you of their status. If you have a device plugged into your serial port, to use in place of the standard keyboard or mouse, it can be set up through this tab.

Summary

- You can configure your system to suit your way of working through the components of the Control Panel.

- Use the Fonts folder to view fonts, remove unwanted ones and install new ones.

- Use Add/Remove Programs to add or remove the components of application suites and of Windows.

- Sounds can be attached to events to alert you to them.

- Use the Mouse panel to set the double-click response and the speed at which the mouse moves the pointer. New pointer icons can be selected here.

- Test and adjust the response rate of the keyboard through the Keyboard panel.

- If several people use the PC, you can set up and configure separate, secure user accounts for them.

- If your PC displays the wrong date or time, adjust it through the Date/Time panel.

- You can set up the keyboard to allow text input in other languages.

- The Accessibility options can make the keyboard easier to use and the screen easier to see.

09

the taskbar and start menu

In this chapter you will learn

- how to control the Taskbar display
- how to create your own Taskbar toolbars
- how to make your system more accessible
- how to customize the Start menu

Aims of this chapter

By now you should be familiar with using the Taskbar and Start menu in your Windows sessions. Here we will look at ways in which you can customize the Taskbar and reorganize the Start menu. The techniques are simple and worth learning – these are two elements of the Windows system that you use regularly, so you should have them set up to your way of working.

9.1 Taskbar options

The Properties panel for the Taskbar and Start Menu can be opened by right-clicking on the Taskbar or the Start button and selecting **Properties**.

The **Taskbar** has seven on/off options. You can see the effects, as you set them, in the preview pane. The first five relate to the overall appearance of the Taskbar.

- **Lock the taskbar** – fixes the current position of the Taskbar and of its toolbars. Unlock it if you want to adjust the layout.

- **Auto hide** – if set, the Taskbar slides off-screen when not in use. Pointing off the screen makes it pop-up again.

- **Keep the taskbar on top of other windows** – will ensure that it is visible no matter how you move windows on screen.

- **Group similar taskbar buttons** – if you have several copies of a program running, e.g. My Computer open at several folders, and the Taskbar is getting crowded, the copies will be piled onto one button. Click to open it up into a list, then select the copy that you want to use.

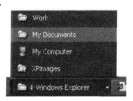

With a small screen, turn on **Auto hide** to maximize the working area.

Figure 9.1 Setting the Taskbar options.

- **Show Quick Launch** – displays the Quick Launch toolbar (see page 6) next to the Start button.

The other two options relate to the **Notification area**. This holds icons for those utility programs that run in the background, such as the volume control, modem or printer.

- **Show clock** – displays the clock in the far right of the Taskbar. Note that if you point to the clock, the date will pop up.

- **Hide inactive icons** – frees up Taskbar space by hiding the icons for those services that are not in use at the time. Click the **Customize** button if you want to see or control which icons are displayed in this area.

9.2 Toolbars

In its initial settings, the Taskbar will have two toolbars on it – **Quick Launch** and **Language Bar**. More can be added if you want to be able to start applications from the Taskbar. There are five ready-made toolbars.

- **Address** – enter a Web address here, and Internet Explorer will start and try to connect to it.

- **Links** – carries a set of buttons with Internet addresses, clicking one starts Internet Explorer to make the connection.

- **Language Bar** – for switching the keyboard settings between different languages.

- **Desktop** – contains copies of the icons present on the Desktop.

- **Quick Launch** – for starting the main Internet applications.

Right-click on a blank area of the Taskbar to open the short menu

Figure 9.2 The Taskbar with the Language Bar and Desktop toolbar. Click the arrows on the right to display the rest of a toolbar's items.

Toolbar options

The short menu that can be opened from a toolbar contains the usual Taskbar items, plus a small set of options that control the appearance of the toolbar.

View – **Large** or **Small** sets the icon size.

Open Folder – opens the toolbar's folder so that you can add or remove shortcuts.

Show Text – adds labels to the program icons.

Show Title – shows the toolbar's title.

Close Toolbar – takes it off the Taskbar.

Creating new toolbars

If you like working from the Taskbar, you can set up one or more toolbars containing shortcuts to your favourite applications, folders – or Internet links (see Chapter 10).

To create a new toolbar:

1 Create a folder, within My Documents, and name it 'My Tools' or something similar.
2 Set up shortcuts to the applications or folders. Either:

Select their icons in My Computer or from the Desktop then hold the right button down as you drag them into this folder, and select the **Create Shortcut Here** option.

Or

Copy existing shortcuts from the Start menu – hold down the right button and drag them from the menu into the folder, then select **Copy Here**.

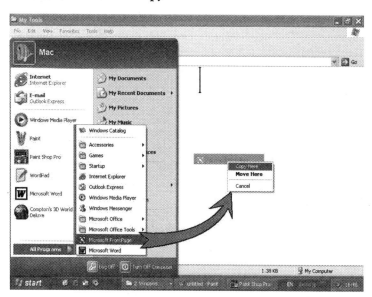

Figure 9.3 Copying a shortcut from the Start menu for the new toolbar. Note that you must hold down the *right button!* If you drag with the left button down, you will remove the items from the Start menu.

3 If you are going to show text labels on the toolbar, edit the names so that they are as brief as possible or you will have trouble displaying them all.

Figure 9.4 The new toolbar folder, almost ready to be added to the Taskbar – most of the names could do with editing.

4 When you have assembled your shortcuts, right-click on the **Taskbar**, point to **Toolbars** and select **New Toolbar...**

5 Work through the folder display to find the one containing your shortcuts.

6 Click **OK**.

Figure 9.5 Adding the new toolbar. You could create several toolbars, one for each of the PC's users, or to suit the different kinds of work that you do on the machine.

9.3 Moving and resizing

The Taskbar is normally a thin bar across the bottom of the screen, and this works very well when it is used only for the Quick Launch toolbar and a few application buttons. Add more toolbars and it is going to get crowded and difficult to use. There are two possible solutions:

- Make the Taskbar deeper by dragging its top edge upwards. The toolbars can be rearranged within this area by dragging on their handles. Move them up or down between the lines, or drag sideways to adjust their relative sizes.

Drag the edge to change the depth

Drag on a dotted handle to move a toolbar or to make it wider/narrower

- Move the Taskbar to one or other side of the screen. By default it will be wide enough to show the Text labels on the icons. You will probably need to adjust the layout by dragging on the handles between the sections, and may want to make the bar slimmer – drag its edge inwards.

Do you need labels?

If the icons are clear enough, the toolbar titles and shortcut labels are not really necessary. Turning them off will save a lot of space, allowing you to pack more into a slim Taskbar.

141

the taskbar and start menu 09

9.4 The Start menu

Right-click on the **Start** button and select **Properties** from the short menu, to go to the **Start Menu** tab of the **Taskbar and Start Menu Properties** panel. Here you can customize the appearance of the menu, and control which items appear on your menu system, and where.

Figure 9.6
The Start Menu
Properties panel.

The Start menu can
be run in XP or
Classic style

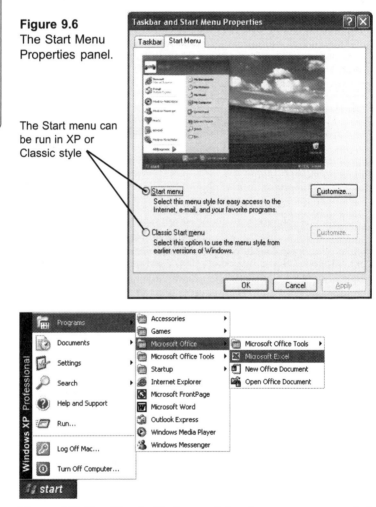

Figure 9.7 The Classic Start menu takes less screen space, but doesn't offer the same quick access to your most-used programs.

The most dramatic change you can make to the menu is to switch to the 'Classic' style – combine this with a Windows Classic screen display and you will have a PC which looks very similar to one running Windows 98. The Classic menu can be customized in just the same way as it can be in earlier versions of Windows, with special routines for adding and removing menu items.

Customizing the Start menu

There are some simple, and some slightly more complicated, things you can do to customize the Start menu. We'll begin with the easy stuff!

1 Click **Customize...**
2 At the **Customize Start Menu** dialog box, start by selecting the icon size.
3 In the **Programs** area you can set how many shortcuts to have in the quick access set on the left – you may want more or less.
4 You can select the programs to run from the **Internet** and the **E-mail** shortcuts, or turn them off if not wanted.

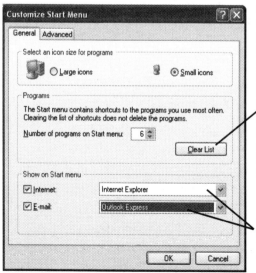

When you first explore XP, you'll probably run some programs that you will rarely reuse later – and they will be added to the list. Clear the list and have a fresh start when you are ready to get down to some serious work.

The shortcuts can link to any suitable programs

Figure 9.8 First steps in customizing the Start menu.

5   On the **Advanced** tab you control which of the standard shortcuts are displayed on the right side of the
menu. All can be turned off if not required. Work
through the **Start menu items** list, setting items to
be displayed or not.

6   Click **OK**.

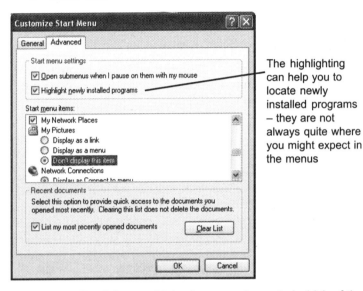

The highlighting
can help you to
locate newly
installed programs
– they are not
always quite where
you might expect in
the menus

Figure 9.9 The **Advanced** tab allows you to control which of the
standard shortcuts are displayed.

Tidying the Start menu shortcuts

If you want to remove a single item from the 'most used'
program shortcuts, open the Start menu, right-click on the
shortcut and select the **Remove from This List** option.

Reorganizing the menus

The Start menu system is stored as a set of folders and subfolders
– or rather, as several sets, as each user has his or her own Start
menu. Within the Start menu are folders for each submenu,
and the shortcuts are held as files in these.

If you have installed so many applications that the **All Programs** menu has become overcrowded, create group folders and move the shortcuts and folders of related applications into these. A short main menu that leads to two levels of submenus is easier to work with than one huge menu!

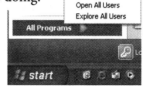

1   Open the Start menu, right-click on **All Programs** then select **Open** from the short menu.

2   When the Start menu folder opens, click **Folders** to display the folder list – it will make it much easier to see what you are doing.

3   Reorganize the menu, using the normal file management techniques for moving, deleting and renaming files (shortcuts) and folders (submenus).

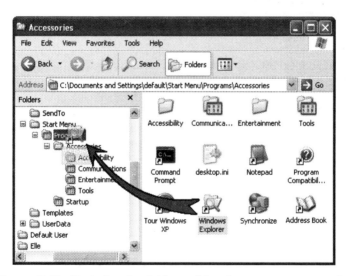

Figure 9.10 Exploring the folders of the Start menu system. In the example, Windows Explorer is being moved to the main **Programs** menu – this is a useful program and should be easy to get to.

Summary

◆ The Taskbar can be displayed on top of all other windows, behind them, or tucked off screen when not in use.

◆ Ready-made toolbars can be added to the Taskbar.

◆ You can create your own folders of shortcuts and turn them into Taskbar toolbars.

◆ You can adjust the depth and position of the Taskbar, and move the toolbars within it.

◆ You can customize the appearance and the selection of shortcuts on the Start menu.

◆ The menu structure can be reorganized using the normal file management techniques.

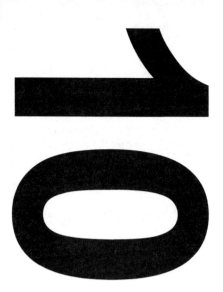

10

internet explorer

In this chapter you will learn

- about the Internet and the World Wide Web
- how to get online and set up Internet Explorer
- how IE can make browsing simpler and faster
- how to save text and images from the Web
- about Internet radio stations

Aims of this chapter

This chapter concentrates on the practical aspects of getting online through Windows XP, and on setting up and using Internet Explorer. We will have a brief look at some of the facilities that can be reached through the Internet, but there isn't room in this book to tackle this huge area properly. If you want to know more about the Internet, try *Teach Yourself The Internet*.

10.1 What is the Internet?

The Internet is a world-wide communications network, linking thousands of computer networks, through a mixture of private and public phone lines and microwave links. Its component networks are run by government agencies, universities and commercial organizations, working co-operatively and loosely controlled by the Internet Society. These organizations bring many millions of people onto the Internet, and millions more link in their home computers through one or other of the many service providers.

At the time of writing, Spring 2003, there are well over 30 million host computers supplying services and information over the Net, and the number of users is estimated to be well over 300 million. In the UK alone, there are over 400,000 host computers on the Internet, and around half of the population has access either from home, or through their work or through their school or university.

The Internet can be accessed and used in a number of ways. For most people, the most important aspects of the Internet are the World Wide Web, electronic mail and newsgroups. Once you get into it, you will soon discover that there are other ways to use the Internet and you might want to investigate some of these over time.

The World Wide Web

This is probably the most exciting and useful aspect of the Internet for most users. It consists of hundreds of millions of *pages* of information, stored on host computers throughout the world. The pages contain text, graphics, video clips, sounds and – most importantly – *hyperlinks* to other pages. Clicking on a hyperlink will take you to another page, which may be in the same computer, or in one a thousand miles away.

Some Web pages are excellent sources of information in their own right, some are treasure troves of links to other valuable pages; and some are pure trivia. You have to be selective, and you have to keep an eye on the phone bill, for Web browsing is a fascinating, but time-consuming activity.

To access the Web you need a browser, such as Internet Explorer, which can display the text and images, and interpret the links that will take you from one page to another.

Finding stuff

Despite the massive quantity of information that is available on the Web, finding the things that interest you is not usually that difficult. There are several *directories*, which hold large sets of organized links to Web pages – and to other parts of the Internet. Yahoo! (page 166) is probably the best known of these, and is an excellent place at which to start researching a subject. There are also *search engines* where you can hunt for pages that contain given words. They are most useful when you are looking for information on a very specific topic as they can pick out the relevant pages from the millions on the Web. The Search button in Internet Explorer will link you to Excite's search engines (see section 10.5).

Online sales and services

The World Wide Web is becoming a good place to do business. New companies have been started to sell goods over the Web (books, CDs, fancy gifts, and computer hardware and software seem to do best at present) and an increasing number of existing shops and other firms are now marketing their goods and services online. Fraud is a problem on the Internet, but probably no more so than it is in any area where business is done. You can shop and deal as safely over the Internet as you can by mail order or in the high street. It's largely a matter of choosing your firms wisely and avoiding too-good-to-be-true bargains.

Figure 10.1 Microsoft runs an extensive Web site – a great source of information and software with links to many resources beyond its site. Here, as on all Web pages, an underline indicates a hyperlink – clicking on it will make the browser go to another page, and this could be within the site or anywhere at all on the World Wide Web.

Your own Home Page

Almost all Internet service providers offer their subscribers the opportunity to have their own home pages. Some people use the pages as notice boards for their local sports or hobby clubs; some run fan clubs on theirs; some will pull together information and links on a subject, making their home pages into valuable resources for others who share their interests.

If you want to create your own home page, you should have some understanding of *HTML* (HyperText Markup Language) – the coding system behind Web pages. It is not difficult to learn, and you don't need to learn much of it if you use FrontPage Express, or other HTML editor. This will handle the nitty-gritty of the HTML system and let you get on with the job of designing the layout and producing the content.

E-mail

Electronic mail is probably the most widely used of all the Internet facilities – after the novelty of browsing the Web has worn thin, you will still be logging on regularly to collect and send e-mail! E-mail is mainly used for sending plain text messages, but you can also send formatted text, and attach images, sounds and other data files to your messages.

Most e-mail is one-to-one communication, but there are also mail lists that circulate messages to their members. Each of the many hundreds of lists covers a specialist interest, and almost all are open to anyone to join.

Newsgroups

These developed from mail lists, and have much in common with them. There are thousands of newsgroups (over 50,000 at the last count), covering an amazing range of interests, activities and obsessions, from the mundane to the bizarre.

Some newsgroups are very active, with hundreds of new articles every day; others have much lighter traffic. Some groups clearly have members with too much free time and free access to the Internet; in others, the articles are typically brief but relevant and interesting.

Some groups are moderated – i.e. they have someone to edit submissions and filter out the irrelevant ones. Unmoderated groups on topics that attract obsessives can produce vast quantities of articles that are of little interest to anyone but their authors.

You may not have access to all the Internet's newsgroups. You can only reach those that are handled by the news server at your service provider, and some providers are more selective than others. Some may offer you the option of accessing only those that are suitable for family audiences – an option worth considering if children use your Internet connection.

10.2 Getting online

Windows XP has all the software that you need to access the Internet. To actually get online from home, you will also need:

* a modem – to convert computer signals into a form that can be sent down the phone lines. If your PC is not already equipped with one, a modem is easily added. Expect to pay around £100 for a fast (56K) modem, or half as much for a 28.8K modem. (The Internet's connections are often so busy that faster modems rarely get the chance to run at full speed!)

* a phone socket within reach of your computer.

* an account with an ISP (Internet Service Provider). This gives you access to the Internet and an e-mail address.

If you have just bought a new Windows XP PC, it will almost certainly have a built-in modem and the software to connect you to an ISP. Unless there are special reasons otherwise, you may as well use the recommended ISP for your first ventures into the Internet. It is not difficult to change ISPs – normally the biggest bother is letting all your contacts know your new e-mail address!

New Connection Wizard

This can be used to find a service provider or to set up a connection to an existing provider. As with all wizards, work through it stage by stage, supplying information or making choices in response to prompts.

* If you are in doubt about anything, accept the default settings.

* Leave all settings at their defaults unless your ISP tells you otherwise.

* If you think you have made a mistake at any stage, click the **Back** button to check and correct earlier entries – or if it's a really crucial mistake, click **Cancel** and start again!

* If you are going to use this to find a provider, you will need persistence and patience. It can take many attempts before you get through to Microsoft's online referral service, where the list of providers is kept!

* If you have already set up an account with a provider, make sure that you have at hand any information they sent to you – including their phone number and your user details. You will also need to know the mail and news servers' names when you go on to set up Outlook Express (see Chapter 11).

- You will be offered the chance to set up your mail, news and Internet directory service. Mail and news are worth doing. The directory service could well be left until later.

You should find the Wizard in the **Programs ➡ Accessories ➡ Communications** submenu of the **Start** menu.

You should not need the area code for a local number

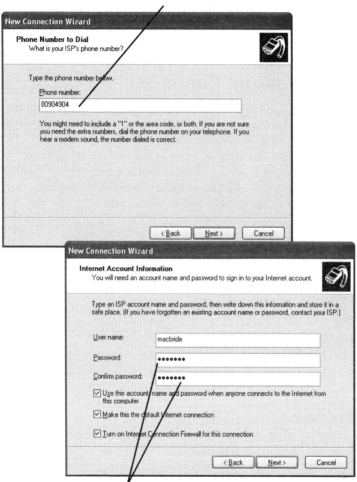

Your user name and password will be stored, so that you can login automatically in future

Figure 10.2 Two stages (of many) from the New Connection Wizard.

Trouble connecting?

If you have any difficulties in establishing a working connection with your provider, look in the Help pages for the Modem Troubleshooter. It will show you what to check, and what to try to solve the problem. If that fails, ring your provider's technical support line – patience is a virtue with most of these.

10.3 Internet Explorer

You can access the Internet from many places in the Windows XP system, but the main tool for this job is Internet Explorer. It is very similar to Windows Explorer or My Computer – especially when using Web page view. In fact, if you use the Favorites, Links buttons or Address bar to connect to an Internet site through either Windows Explorer or My Computer, they will effectively turn into Internet Explorer.

*   Microsoft would like you to view the Internet as an extension of your Desktop. If you connect through an ISDN line, or better still a fast, high-capacity leased line that is permanently open, then this may be a viable view. If you connect by dialling in to a service provider, the transition from Desktop to Internet will rarely be smooth.

For the rest of this chapter, I'll concentrate on Internet Explorer, but it's worth bearing in mind that this is not the only route into the Net.

Internet Explorer is designed for fast, easy navigation, both on and offline. When you browse a page, its files are stored in a temporary folder on your hard disk. When you return to the same page, its files are then loaded from the disk, rather than downloaded from the Internet. This makes browsing far, far quicker! We all have our own favourite places that we use to start searching for stuff, and when following up links you will often find pages with several good leads, and you will want to return to these to pick up new trails.

These stored files also allow you to 'revisit' sites when you are offline, but it should be noted that this does not always work.

Some pages insist on downloading new files – typically adverts – each time they are opened, and will not display without them.

The Internet Explorer window

- The **Standard**, **Address** and **Links toolbars** can be turned on or off – the Address (page 165) is more useful here than it is in Windows Explorer.

- The **Explorer Bar** can display Search (page 164), Favorites (page 168), Media (page 173) or History (page 167).

- For maximum viewing area when browsing, switching to **Full Screen View** will turn off all the features of the window, except the Standard toolbar.

Explorer Bar options

Forward   Refresh   Search   Media   Mail
Back   \   Stop   \   Home   /   Favorites / History   Print

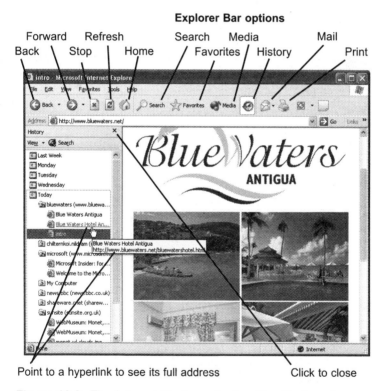

Point to a hyperlink to see its full address   Click to close

Figure 10.3 The Internet Explorer display. The Explorer bar on the left can be opened to display the History list (pages visited recently), Favorites, a Search facility or online Media.

The Standard toolbar

These buttons contain almost all of the controls that you need
when you are online.

* **Back** and **Forward** move between the pages already visited
during the session.

* **Stop** – use it when you realize at the start of a long download
that you don't really want to see that page.

* **Refresh** redraws the current page.

* **Home** goes to your start page – your jumping off point
into the Web. This can be your own home page or any other.

* The **Explorer bar** buttons open the bar to run a Search, or
browse the Favorites or the History folders.

* **Full Screen** toggles between Full Screen and normal view.

* **Mail** starts or switches to your mail software (normally Outlook Express) for reading or sending e-mail or newsgroups
(see Chapter 11).

* **Print** prints the current page (text and graphics).

Menu commands

Most of the ones that you will use regularly are duplicated by
the Toolbar buttons, and are better handled through them.
However, there are some very useful commands that can only
be reached through the menus:

* **File** ➡ **New** ➡ **Window** opens a second browser window, so
that you can keep one page at hand while you follow up
other leads.

* **File** ➡ **Work Offline** should be turned on when using Explorer offline.

* **Edit** ➡ **Find** will search for words in the current page.

* **View** ➡ **Text size** lets you set the size of the text (headlines
are scaled to match).

File ➡ **Open**, **Tools** ➡ **Internet Options** and the **Add** and
Organize Favorites commands are also important. We will return to them later in this chapter.

10.4 Internet Options

These options can be set or changed at any time on or offline (though the odd couple only take effect after you restart the PC). A few should be set before you start to use Explorer in earnest, others are best left until you have been using it for a while and have a clearer idea of what settings best suit your preferred way of working.

- Use **Tools ➡ Internet Options** to open the panel, and click on the tab names to move between the sets of options.

- If you set options that change the appearance of the screen, click **Apply** to see how they look.

- Only click **OK** when you have finished with all the tabs.

General

The **Home page** defines where Explorer goes when it is first started. This could be a personalized start page at Microsoft (or other content provider – many offer this facility), your own home page, or a blank page if each session is a new voyage. An address can be typed in here, but it is simpler to wait until you are online at the right place, then just come back to this tab and click **Use Current**.

In **Temporary Internet files**, click **Settings...** to define how Explorer should handle page files.

- In the **Check for newer version of stored pages**, select *Every visit to the page*, if the pages you use a lot change frequently.

- The **Amount of disk space to use** depends upon how much browsing you do, how often you return to pages and how much space you have. When the space is used up, older files are wiped to make way for new ones. A typical page of text and graphics might add up to 50Kb – say 20 pages per Mb. How many pages do you want in store – remembering that, if you update pages when you revisit, those that you use regularly will be relatively new files.

- If you have more spare space on a second hard disk, click **Move Folder** and set up the temporary storage space there.

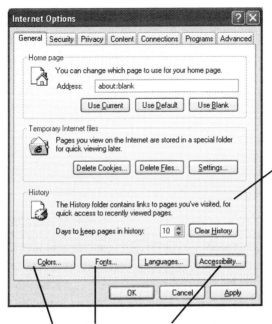

The History records your movements, to allow easier revisiting – how long do you want to keep it?

Set the Colors, Fonts and Accessibility options if you need a high visibility display.

If you tend to visit pages that have a lot of images or information, and want to be able to study these later, offline, set a high disk space level.

Figure 10.4 Setting the **General** options.

Security and privacy

The Internet is basically a safe place – as long as you take a few sensible precautions. If you spend most of your time at major commercial and other well-established sites, and at ones they recommend, security should not be a major concern. If you browse more widely, you may bump up against the mischievous and the unscrupulous. The main dangers are these:

* **Viruses** – You can only get these by running executable files (programs) or macros in documents. You cannot pick up a virus simply by browsing a page or reading e-mail or news articles. A virus-checker will give you an extra level of protection.

* **Active content** – Web designers may use small programs (applets), written in Java, Javascript or ActiveX to enhance their pages – though many are just decorative. The languages are designed to be secure – the programs should not be able to access your system – but hackers do find loopholes.

* **Privacy intrusions** – Every time you fill in a form online, run a search or make a choice, you send some information about yourself along with the intended data. Some sites may attempt to store and misuse this information.

* **Cookies** – A cookie is a short file, written by a site onto your hard disk. They are normally used to store your personal preferences at that site – so that when you revisit you don't have to set preferences again – or simply to log your visit. There are different sorts of cookies, some more intrusive than others. On the **Privacy** tab, you can set your limits for accepting cookies.

Zones and security levels

On the Security tab, you will find that IE sorts sites into four zones: *Local intranet*, *Trusted sites*, *Restricted sites* and *Internet* (everything else). The default levels have already been set for these. At first, either do not change them or nudge the levels a little higher.

Later, when you are more aware of what you are likely to meet and how you like to use the Internet, you may like to use the **Custom Level** to define how IE is to respond to sites in each zone.

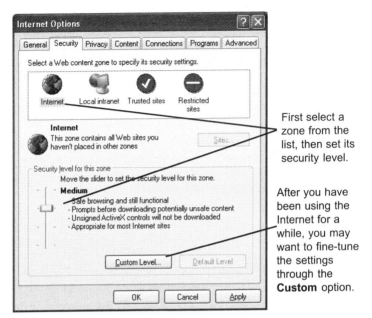

First select a zone from the list, then set its security level.

After you have been using the Internet for a while, you may want to fine-tune the settings through the **Custom** option.

Figure 10.5 The **Security** tab – when in doubt, play safe!

With the highest level of security you will find that some sites will not let you in. The **Advanced** options allow you to set up IE so that you can decide whether or not to accept cookies which would otherwise be blocked.

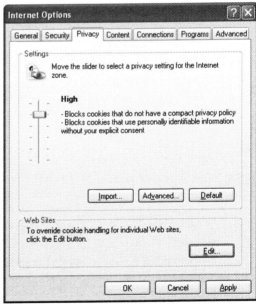

Figure 10.6 Using the **Privacy** tab to control cookies.

Content Advisor and safe surfing

If children can get online from your PC, you may want to enable the Content Advisor to set limits to the types of material that they can access through the Internet.

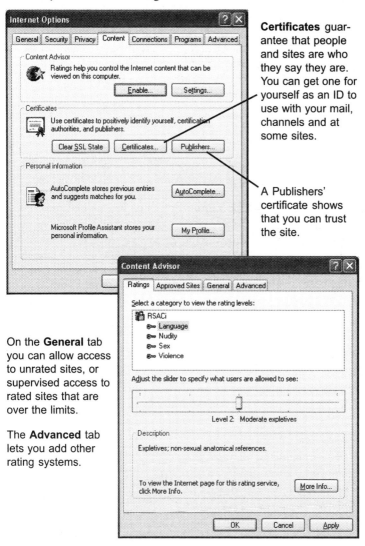

Certificates guarantee that people and sites are who they say they are. You can get one for yourself as an ID to use with your mail, channels and at some sites.

A Publishers' certificate shows that you can trust the site.

On the **General** tab you can allow access to unrated sites, or supervised access to rated sites that are over the limits.

The **Advanced** tab lets you add other rating systems.

Figure 10.7 The **Content** tab. Turn on **Content Advisor** if you are going to let children have unsupervised access to the Internet.

The Content Advisor allows you to restrict unsupervised access to those sites which have been rated by the Recreational Software Advisory Council for the Internet (RASCi). This rates sites on a scale of 1 to 5 for language, nudity, sex and violence. You set the limits of what may be accessed from your machine.

Many perfectly acceptable sites do not have a rating, simply because they have not applied for one, but this is not a major problem. It just means that the kids will have to ask someone who knows the password to override the restrictions when they find somewhere good but unrated. And if you want to browse unrestricted, you can disable the advisor.

Safer surfing

If you are concerned about people reaching the murkier corners of the Internet, Content Advisor is only the first line of defence. For more about child safety, browse over to **http://www.safekids.com**.

Advanced

Most of the **Advanced** options should be left well alone until you really know what you are doing, but there are a couple that you might want to look at now.

In the **Accessibility** section, turning on **Always expand ALT text for images** will make sure that there is enough space to display all the ALT text if **Show Pictures** has been turned off.

At the bottom of the **Browsing** section, turn on **Use inline AutoComplete** if you want IE to try to finish URLs for you when you start typing them into the Address bar – this is a very handy facility.

In the **Multimedia** section, turn off the **Play** options for faster browsing. Turning **Show Pictures** off will also improve downloading times, but pictures often carry essential information and hyperlinks. With **Show Pictures** off, you can download an individual picture by clicking on the ▧ which appears in its place.

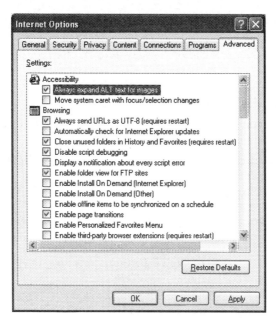

Figure 10.8 Most **Advanced** options should be left at their defaults
– click **Restore Defaults** if you think you may have messed them up!

10.5 Browsing the Web

Hypertext links provide an efficient means of following threads
from page to page, but with so much information spread over
so many pages on so many sites over the Web, the problem is
where to start looking.

Your Internet Service Provider's home site will probably offer a
directory with an organized set of links to selected sites, and
Internet Explorer is initially set up to head to MSN (MicroSoft
Network). This has a good directory, and a useful search facility. You may as well leave it as your start point until you have
found a better place, then change to its address in the Internet
Options dialog box (page 157).

The directory approach is good for starting research on general topics, but if you are looking for specific material, you are
often better off running a search, and with Internet Explorer
you can run a search at any time, no matter where you are on
the Web.

Running a search

1 Click 🔍 Search to start the Search in the Explorer bar.

2 Type a word or phrase to describe what you are looking for.

3 Click the **Search** button.

4 When you get the results, click on a link to view the page in the main window.

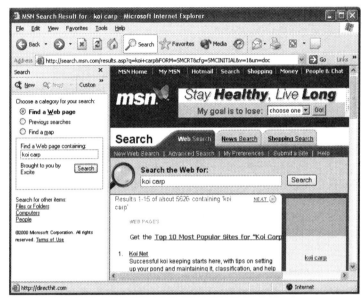

Figure 10.9 The main panel shows MSN's Web search page. A search here and one at Excite (run in the Explorer bar) would produce different, but overlapping, sets of results. Every 'search engine' has its own way of finding and indexing sites, but some sites are very good at making sure that all the searches find them!

Uniform Resource Locators (URL)

With all the millions of Web pages, files and other resources that can be reached over the Internet, a standardized way of identifying them is essential. URLs provide this. There are different styles of URL for each approach to the Internet, though they all follow much the same pattern:

type://hostcomputer/directory/filename

Web pages

Many of these are instantly recognizable from their *html* or *htm* endings, which shows that they are hypertext pages.

http://sunsite.unc.edu/boutell/faq/www-faq.html

This one is a list of frequently asked questions (*faq*) and their answers, about the World Wide Web (*www*), stored in the Sun archives in the University of North Carolina (*unc*).

The URL of the top page of a site may just consist of the site address, with an (optional) slash at the end. This is the opening page at Microsoft's site:

http://www.microsoft.com/

If you know the URL of a page, you can jump directly to it.

Use **File ➡ Open**, and type the URL into the panel, or type it into the **Address** toolbar.

The leading **http://** is not essential. Browsers expects you to enter a World Wide Web URL. Thus:

http://uk.yahoo.com

can be entered as:

uk.yahoo.com

URLs must be typed exactly right for the routine to work. They are not case-sensitive – UK.YAHOO.COM works just as well as uk.yahoo.com – but watch out for symbols. Some URLs include a tilde (~). Where the URL is for the top page of a site, it will end with a slash (/). This can be omitted.

Finding URLs

Before you can use a URL, you have to know it. There are several possible sources:

♦ As you browse the Web, you may find a hyperlink to a page that you do not want to visit at the time, but might like to drop in on later. Point to it, to display its URL in the Status bar, and make a note of it.

♦ If you join any **newsgroups** (Chapter 11), you will often
see notices about relevant pages on the newsgroup area of
interest, particularly new ones.

♦ Internet magazines and newspaper columns often have
'What's new' features.

Other start points

There are many places that you can use as start points for your
surfing. Some that are well worth a visit include:

♦ Yahoo!'s main site – the original and probably still the best
of the directories, at

http://www.yahoo.com

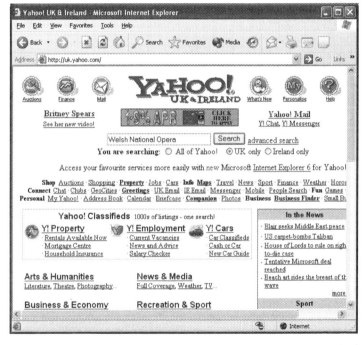

Figure 10.10 There are local Yahoo!s in many countries, backed
up by the central directory at www.yahoo.com. Yahoo! also offers
e-mail, news, weather, shopping and auctions, games and more.

- ◆ Yahoo! UK & Ireland, at
  http://uk.yahoo.com or http://www.yahoo.co.uk
- ◆ Excite offers an excellent directory, search and more, at
  http://www.excite.co.uk
- ◆ The most comprehensive, but also the fastest, search engine is Google, at
  http://www.google.com
- ◆ Another excellent search engine is AltaVista, at
  http://altavista.digital.com

But before you can get to these, you need to know about URLs. Read on!

History

When you want to return to a page, the simplest way is through the Back button and its drop-down list. This only works with those visited very recently – the Back list is wiped at the end of a session, and can be corrupted by movements within sites,

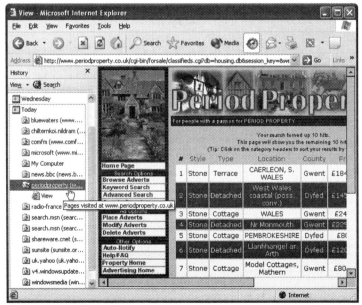

Figure 10.11 Using the **History** list. Pages are grouped into their sites, making it easier to find them again.

especially those with complex, interactive page layouts. The most reliable way to revisit pages is by opening the History list in the Explorer Bar. The pages are grouped by day and then by site, making it easy to find the one you want.

Favorites

The Explorer Bar can also be used to display the Favorites list. This has a few sets of ready-made links, but is really intended as a store of links to those places that you like to visit regularly.

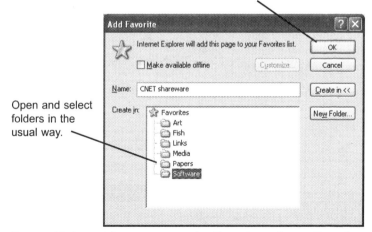

* When you find a page that you will want again in future, open the **Favorites** menu and select **Add to Favorites** or open **Favorites** in the Explorer Bar and click **Add...**

* Edit the name, if necessary – the page's title will be suggested.

* If you want to store the link in a folder, go to the **Create in:** list and choose it – a new folder can be created, if needed.

* Click **OK**.

If you are in a hurry, click OK, leaving the name as given. The link will be added to the main list. You can move it and rename it later.

Open and select folders in the usual way.

Figure 10.12 Adding a page to the **Favorites**. If your Favorites folders get crowded, use **Organize Favorites** to open a display of the folders. You can then move, rename and delete the stored links.

10.6 Files from the Net

Shareware sites

One of the great things about the Internet is that you can get from it virtually all the tools that you need to work on the Net. You already have a browser, of course, but there are more tools that you may like to acquire. The Internet is also a great source of games, audio/video clips, pictures, text files and more.

If you are looking for software, try these excellent shareware sites, both run by c|net – shareware.com (**http://www. shareware.com**) and download.com (**http://www.download. com**). Here you can search by keyword or program, or browse by category. When you find something that you want, clicking on the program's name will start the download – decide which folder to store it in, and sit back and wait. Downloading speeds vary, but average around 100Kb per minute.

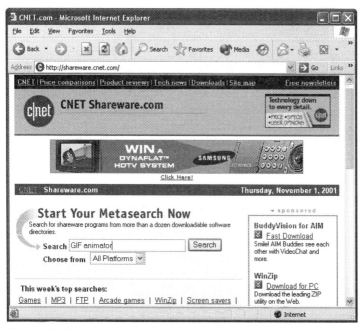

Figure 10.13 shareware.com – a great source of software. Some of it is free, the rest is shareware – try it for free, but pay a (small) fee to continue using it.

ZIPped files

Many of the files available over the Internet are compressed to save space. This can reduce file sizes, and therefore transfer times, by up 90%. Zipped files can be opened in My Computer.

Saving pages and images

You can revisit a page, offline, for as long as it is kept in the temporary files area, but if you want a permanent copy of a page you should save it.

* Wait until the page is fully loaded, then open the **File** menu and select **Save As** – you may need to change the filename to something more memorable. If you set the **Save as type** to *Web Page complete*, then any images and the component files of framed pages will be saved in a folder with the same name as the page.

Figure 10.14 Saving a Web page. If you just want the text of a simple page, set the **Save as type** to Web Page, HTML only. Use Web Page complete if you want to save all the associated files.

* When you want to view the page again, use **File** ➜ **Open**, then browse through your folders to locate it.

If you don't want the whole page, but just an individual image from it, this can be saved separately.

* Point anywhere on the picture and wait for the image toolbar to appear, then click the **Save this image** button.

* If you like the image and it is big enough to make a good background for your Desktop, right-click on it and select **Set as background** from the short menu.

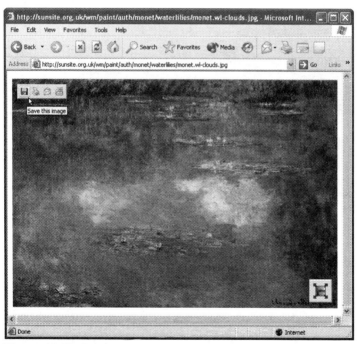

Figure 10.15 Saving an image off a Web page. If you like art, try the Web Museum. There are 'mirror' copies of this at many sites, including **http://sunsite.org.uk/wm**.

Windows Update

Windows XP comes with an automatic update system. This will check the Microsoft Web site regularly, when you are online, to see if there are updates available that you should have. If there are, the system will download and install them for you. You don't need to do anything about this – it just happens! If you prefer to control when and how your Windows software is updated, you can turn this facility off – open **Automatic Updates** in the Control Panel and switch to manual control.

If you choose to update manually, or want to see what optional updates are available, click on the **Windows Update** shortcut on the main **Start** menu. This is a highly automated page. It has routines that will check over your system to see if there are any files for which new replacements or 'patch' repairs are available. If there are any – or if you find any optional add-ons that you would like – they will be downloaded and installed for you.

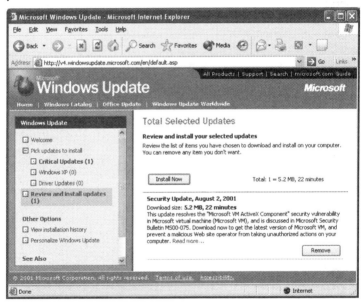

Figure 10.16 The Windows Update page. My system has just been checked, and it seems that I need the **Critical Updates** package. Clicking **Install Now** will get that and install it for me.

10.7 Internet radio

Want some music while you are surfing? Then turn the radio on! You can now listen to radio broadcasts from all over the world through your PC. Here's how:

1 Click the **Media** button to open Media in the Explorer Bar.

2 Click the **Media Options** button at the bottom of the bar and select **Radio Guide**. This will take you to WindowsMedia, where they have links to radio stations all over the world.

3 Pick a **Featured Station**, or click **Find More Stations** to explore and choose from their huge selection.

♦ A small window will open for the broadcast, and – usually – another for the station's site. You do not have to keep it open to listen. You can start it playing then surf on else-where.

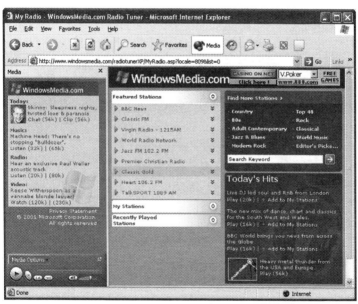

Figure 10.17 Setting up a new radio station. Stations can be added to your **My Stations** list, and picked from there when you use Radio Guide in future, or added to your **Favorites** – this will give you a quicker, direct link to the station.

Easy listening?

The radio sound quality is generally good, but continuity can be a problem. New compression techniques have greatly reduced the size of sound files, but they still take quite a bit of telephone line capacity, and there's not much to spare. If you get online through an ISDN line, you'll have no problem. If you link through a dial-up connection, data comes in from the Web at rarely more than 2Kb per second. That's about enough to cope with a broadcast, but if you are also surfing elsewhere, that will add to the overall quanitity of data trying to come in. Expect occasional breaks in transmission of a second or so, and expect other sites to download more slowly.

Figure 10.18 In theory, you can watch TV on the Internet, but first you may have to install RealPlayer as many video broadcasters prefer this format to Media Player. Whatever the player, the pictures are always small and jerky, so, although you can watch the news at **news.bbc.co.uk**, you are actually better off reading it!

Summary

- The Internet is the result of world-wide co-operation between computer networks in commercial, educational and other organizations.

- To get online, you need a modem, a convenient phone line and an account with a service provider.

- The New Connection Wizard can be used to find a provider, or to set up a connection to an existing account.

- Internet Explorer is an integral part of Windows XP.

- Some of the Internet options should be set early on; others can be left until you have spent more time on the Internet.

- If children can get online from your PC, you should enable the Content Advisor.

- The Web consists of pages linked together by URLs given as hyperlinks in the pages.

- Every site on the Internet has its own unique address – its URL (Uniform Resource Locator). If you know the URL of a page, you can jump directly to it.

- Directories help you find your way around; Yahoo! is the most comprehensive of these. Search engines can be used to track down pages containing keywords.

- The Explorer Bar can be used to run an online search, or to open the History or Favorites folders or to play media.

- You can add pages to the Favorites folder, and organize them into your own set of folders.

- Files can be downloaded from many places on the Internet – shareware sites have free and cheap software.

- A Web page can be saved as a file. Pictures can also be saved separately.

- Use Windows Update to keep your system up to date.

- You can listen to the radio through the Internet.

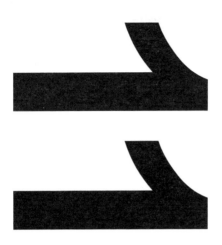

11 outlook express

In this chapter you will learn

- how Outlook Express works
- about sending and receiving e-mail
- about the options in Outlook Express
- how to use the Address Book
- about newsgroups

Aims of this chapter

Outlook Express can handle e-mail or access the newsgroups. In this chapter we will take a look at its main facilities, and cover some of the key points about e-mail and news.

11.1 Starting Outlook Express

Outlook Express can be started from the Desktop icon or the **Programs ➡ Internet Explorer** menu. The initial screen should have the Folder List to the left of the main pane, with its icons for starting the various routines, and the usual toolbar and menu bar above. There are alternative displays – reach them through the **View ➡ Layout** command.

* The **Outlook Bar** can be used as well as, or in place of, the Folder list for moving round the system.

* The **Folder Bar** can be turned on to provide a more substantial heading (it doesn't do anything else).

The Folders

At first, there are only five folders – six if you have the news set up. More can be created to provide organized storage for any mail messages and news articles that you want to retain.

* The **Inbox** holds mail sent to you. The messages remain here, after reading, until you move or delete them.

* The **Outbox** provides temporary storage for messages, while they are waiting to be sent. If you compose your messages offline, you are only online to your service provider for as long as it takes to send them and to collect incoming mail. It doesn't just reduce your costs, it also gives you time to check your text for typing and spelling errors first.

* The **Sent** folder keeps a copy of outgoing messages, if you choose to keep copies (see page 183).

* **Deleted Items** is where messages and articles are stored when they are first deleted. They are only removed completely when deleted from here.

Outlook Bar   Folder Bar   Folder List

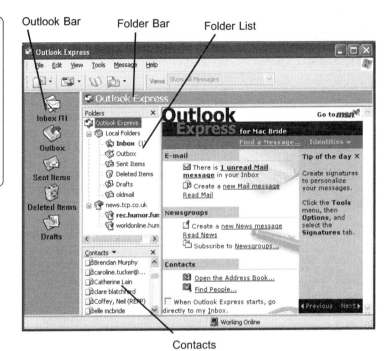

Contacts

Figure 11.1 The **Outlook Express** screen, with the optional elements displayed. Use either the **Outlook Bar** or **Folder List** to move around the system – you do not need both. The Folder Bar is just decorative. The **Contacts** display can be useful, but it is easy enough to get names from the Address Book (page 186) when you need them.

♦ Use **Drafts** as a temporary store for messages that you want to work on some more before sending.

♦ If you have set up a news server, you will have a news folder.

11.2 Reading mail

All mail and news folders follow the same pattern. In the top pane are the message or article headers. These show the name of the sender, its subject and when it was received. They are normally in date order, but can be sorted by sender, subject or date, by clicking on the column name. If the message has not yet been read, its header will be in **bold**. When you select a header, the message is displayed in the preview pane (or in a separate window, if you have chosen this option).

When a message is displayed, these tools are available for dealing with it:

Reply – opens the New Message window, with the sender's name in the **To:** slot, ready to send back to them. This is neat as it means that you do not have to think about their e-mail address.

Reply to all – use this instead of Reply where a message has been mailed to a group of people, and you want your reply to reach the whole group! Your reply will then be mailed to all those who received a **To:** or **Cc:** copy (page 182) of the message.

Forward – copies the message into the New Message window, so that you can send it on to another person. This

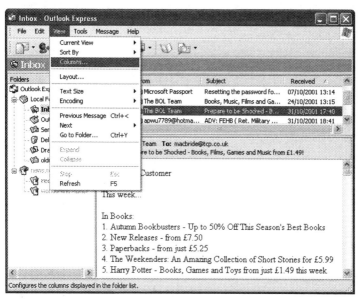

Figure 11.2 The Inbox, with a message in the preview pane. The **View** ➡ **Columns...** option lets you select which items to display in the headers lines, though From, Subject and Received are generally enough to be able to find and sort messages efficiently.

time you will have to supply the address, just as if you were sending a new message – see below.

 Delete – moves the message to the Deleted folder. You can get Outlook Express to empty the Deleted folder for you on exit, or let them stay there, where they can be recovered if necessary – as with the Recycle Bin – until you delete them from there.

+ You can also drag a message, at any time, from the header list to another folder for storage.

When people send you mail, it is stored in your mailbox at your Internet service provider.

If you work in an organization with a permanently open connection to the Internet, you can set up the options (page 182), so that Outlook Express checks the box and downloads new messages for you at set intervals.

If you get online through a dial-up connection, pick up your mail, and send any messages from your Outbox, whenever you are ready.

Click  to send and receive all your mail, or drop down its list (or open the **Tools** menu) if you only want to **Send** or **Receive** at that time.

Send and Receive All Ctrl+M
Receive All
Send All
mail.tcp.co.uk (Default)

11.3 Sending mail

Outlook Express, like most modern mail software, can handle messages in HTML format (as used on Web pages), as well as plain text. This means that you can use different fonts, sizes and colours for your text, set bulleted or numbered lists and other layout options, and insert pictures. If you want colourful messages, without the bother of formatting them, there are a dozen Stationery styles. These give you decorative backgrounds and some also have matching text formats already set.

+ Don't waste time formatting messages if the person to whom you are writing can only read plain text on their system.

To write and send a message:

1 Click the **New Message** button, or use the menu command **Message** ➡ **New Message**.

181
outlook express
11

Or

2 Open the New Message drop-down list, or select **Message** ➡ **New Message Using** and pick your Stationery from the list.

If you decide you don't like the Stationery, **Format** ➡ **Apply Stationery** will let you choose another style, or revert to a plain background.

3 When the Compose window opens, either type the recipient's e-mail address into the **To:** box, or click **To:** and select it from your Address Book (see page 186 for more on this).

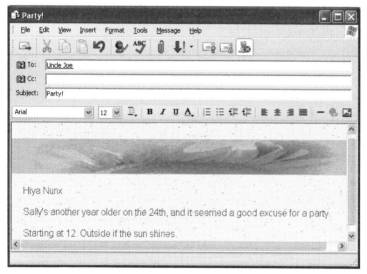

Figure 11.3 Composing a message using the Sunflower stationery – apply formats as in normal word-processing.

4 If more than one person is to get a copy, you can add addresses in the **To:** box (separated by semicolons or commas), or put them in the **Cc:** or **Bcc:** boxes.

To: the main recipients – you would normally expect to get replies from these people.

Cc: Carbon copies, sent mainly for information.

Bcc: Blind carbon copies – their names will not appear in the lists of recipients that normally accompany each message. Used for circulating mail to large groups.

5 Type a **Subject** for the message, so that recipients know what it is about when they see the header in their mail window.

6 Type and format your message. If you don't have the spell checker set to run automatically, you should read the message through to check for errors.

7 Click the **Send** button. If the spell checker is turned on, it will run at this point. After you have worked through any errors it finds, the message will be sent immediately, or stored in the Outbox to be sent later – it depends on the settings (see below).

Or

8 If you want to override your default send settings, open the **File** menu and select **Send Message** (i.e. now) or **Send Later**.

11.4 Outlook Express options

As with most software, the optional settings make more sense after you have been using it for a while, and the default settings are usually a safe bet to start with. However, there are a few that are worth checking and setting early on. Use **Tools ➡ Options...** to open the **Options** panel.

The **General** tab deals with the interaction between Outlook Express and your system.

*   Turn on *Check for new messages every ?? minutes*, and set the interval, if you are permanently online or have long online sessions.

*   Turn off *Notify me if there are any new newsgroups* if you don't bother much with the news.

*   All the other options are probably best turned on at this stage.

The **Read** tab is mainly concerned with news articles.

- Some groups have hundreds of articles every day. You can set how many headers to download at a time.

- Where a set of articles has the same Subject (follow-ons start with 'Re:') they are grouped. If *Automatically expand grouped messages* is off, only the first is shown until you click ⊞.

The **Receipts** tab controls how you deal with receipts – you can request them when sending messages, and people may ask for them from you.

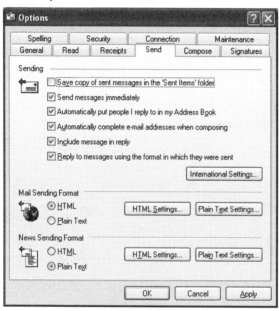

Figure 11.4 The **Send** options.

The **Send** tab is mainly about message formats, see Figure 11.4.

- Turn on *Save copy of sent messages* only if you normally need to keep a copy for later reference.

- Turn on *Send messages immediately* if you normally deal with your mail online.

- Turning on *Automatically put people I reply to in my Address Book* is a good idea. It ensures that their address is correct – as it has been copied from their mail. If this includes some people you do not want, they can easily be removed.

- The *Include message in reply* option can be useful, especially if most of your e-mail is work-related. When replying, you can edit out any unwanted bits of the original message.

- Set your **Mail Sending Format** to *HTML* if most of your recipients are able to read HTML formatted messages, but select *Plain Text* for News.

The **Compose** tab lets you define your message format, setting the default fonts and stationery.

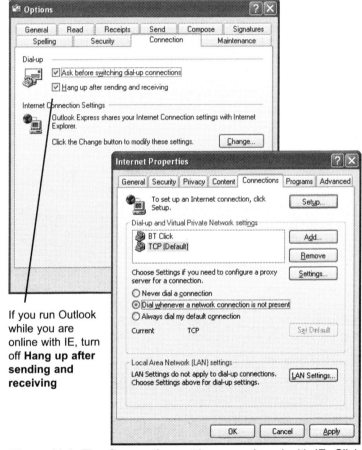

If you run Outlook while you are online with IE, turn off **Hang up after sending and receiving**

Figure 11.5 The **Connection** settings are shared with IE. Click **Change** to reach the Internet Properties dialog box. Selecting *Dial whenever a network connection is not present* will set it dialling (if needed) when you try to go to a Web site or send and receive mail.

The **Spelling** tab controls the way that the spell checker works. The main option is *Always check spelling before sending* – turn this on or off. Other options let you select the dictionary and define the kind of words that the spell checker should ignore.

The **Security** tab should be left alone for the time being – and can be ignored altogether if you are not bothered about the security of your mail.

The **Maintenance** tab is mainly about cleaning up messages.

* Turn on *Empty messages from the Deleted Items folder on exit* unless you tend to delete items in error regularly. If this is off, you will have to select and delete the messages in the folder yourself to remove them from your system.

* Compacting does not delete messages, but stores them more efficiently. Compacted messages take a fraction longer to open.

* The remaining message options all refer to newsgroup messages. How long – if at all – do you want to keep old

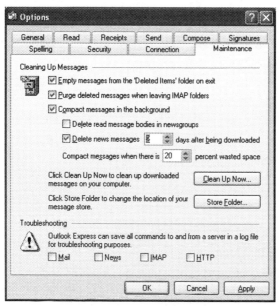

Figure 11.6 Clearing out old messages doesn't just save space – rarely a problem with big modern hard disks – it also makes it far easier to see what's left and find the stuff you really want.

newsgroup articles? Remember that selected messages can be copied to other folders for storage.

• The **Troubleshooting** options can be turned on if you have problems with your mail or news. The log files could provide useful information for whoever tries to solve the problems.

11.5 The Address Book

You must get e-mail addresses exactly right, or the post won't get through. Unfortunately, addresses are not always user-friendly and are rarely easy to remember.

The Address Book is a great idea. Once you have an e-mail address in here – correctly – you need never worry about it again. When you want to write to someone, you can select the name from the book and start to compose from there, or start the message and then select the names at the **To:** and **Cc:** boxes (see page 181).

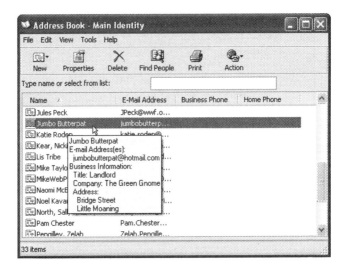

Figure 11.7 My Address Book – you can store phone numbers and 'snail mail' address details here as well. If you do store phone numbers, you can get the Address Book to dial the number for you – the command is in the drop-down **Action** menu.

Adding to the Address Book

1 Open the **Address Book** from the **Tools** menu or click .

2 Click **New** and select **New Contact**. There are tabs for lots of information, but only the **Name** tab is essential.

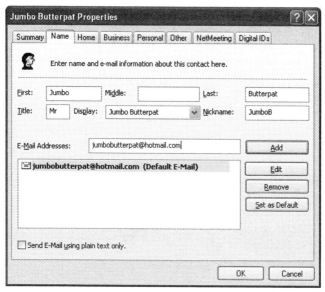

Figure 11.8 Adding a new contact. The first and last names and the e-mail address are the only essentials, and are quickly added.

3 The First, Middle and Last names should be entered separately if you want to be able to sort the list by First and Last names. (**View ➡ Sort By** has a number of alternative sort orders – very useful when you have lots of entries.)

4 A **Nickname** can be entered, if wanted, and either this or the full name can be set as the **Display** value.

5 Type the address *carefully* into the **E-mail address:** box, and click **Add**. If the person has more than one e-mail address, add the others then select one as the default.

6 If you know that the person can only handle plain text on their system, turn on **Send E-Mail using plain text only**.

7 Switch to the other tabs to enter more details if required, then click **OK**.

Copying e-mail addresses

If you have received an e-mail from someone that you want to add to the Address Book, the address can be copied in almost automatically. Start to reply to the person, then right-click on the name in the To: slot. Select **Add To Address Book** from the short menu. The name and e-mail address will be copied into place for you. If you don't actually want to reply to them at that time, just close down the window.

Using the Address Book

If the Address Book is open already, you can start a new message to someone by selecting their name and picking **Send Mail** from the **Action** menu. The **New Message** window will open, with the name in the **To:** box.

If you start from the New Message button, click the 🔳 To: icon to open the **Select Recipients** panel. This lists the names in your Address Book. Pick the recipients one at a time, clicking

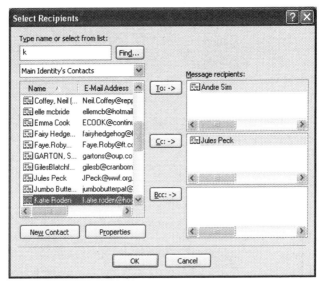

Figure 11.9 Using the **Select Recipients** panel to get addresses from your Address Book. If you add a name by mistake, just select it and press the **Delete** key.

To:->, Cc:-> or Bcc:-> to copy them to the appropriate categories. Click **OK** when you've done. The recipients will appear as
names, rather than e-mail addresses – don't worry. They will be
translated into addresses before sending.

11.6 Finding people

The simplest and safest way to get someone's e-mail address is
to ring them up and ask them to send you an e-mail message.
If this isn't possible, you may be able to find the address in one
of the Internet's people-finding sites. These hold databases of
names and addresses that they have compiled in various ways –
none give complete coverage.

You are more likely to be able to find someone if they get online
through an Internet Service Provider than if they go through a
business or other organization – these are often reluctant to
release internal information to the people-finding databases. If
you are looking for people in the USA, you can probably find
their phone numbers easier than their e-mail addresses, as most
of the sites have the US telephone databases. Having said all
that, it's always worth a try. You may be able to find that long-
lost schoolchum, or Uncle Arthur who emigrated in 1964.

You can run a search at half a dozen of the best sites through
the **Find People** panel.

1 Go online.

2 Open the **Start** menu, point to **Search** and select **People…**

Figure 11.10 Starting a search for an address. If Bigfoot has a
'Tony Blair' in its database, the panel will expand to show the
results.

3 Pick a site from the **Look in** list – it doesn't matter which.

4 Type in the first and last names.

5 Click **Find Now**.

6 If it doesn't work, try different sites. If you still have no joy, try with just the initial and the name – you cannot be sure how they gave their name when they signed up for e-mail. This will produce more unwanted hits for you to sort through.

7 If your search produces too many results, you may be better going to the Web site – click the button to connect to the current **Look in** site. Most have advanced search facilities that will let you define your search more closely.

11.7 Newsgroups

Newsgroups are where people come together to share common interests and enthusiasms, to ask for and give help, to debate and to announce new discoveries and creations. There are over 50,000 of them, each devoted to a different topic, ranging from the seriously academic to the totally trivial. They are organized into about 20 major (and many more minor) divisions, subdivided by topic, and subdivided again where necessary.

Their names reflect this structure and describe their focus; for example, *rec.arts.animation* is found in the *arts* subdivision of the *rec* division and is devoted to *animation* as an art form. (There are other animation groups, with different focuses.)

Most newsgroups belong to one or other of these divisions.

alt – the alternative newsgroups, set up to cover topics that had not been included in the other main divisions. Hobbies, obsessions and fan clubs form a substantial part of the *alt* groups, though there are also groups for professional interests and discussions. As a neat example of the diversity, here are three adjacent groups: *alt.architecture.int-design*, *alt.aromatherapy*, *alt.art.bodypainting*.

biz – business-oriented groups, carrying announcements of new products, jobs and discussions of market-related issues.

comp – a large set of newsgroups covering many aspects of computing, including languages, applications, hardware and standards.

misc – miscellaneous. Books, health, education, kids, for sale adverts and job opportunities make up the bulk of these.

news – among these newsgroups about newsgroups you will find several specially for new users. *news.newusers* is a good source of tips and advice, while *news.answers* may solve your problems.

rec – a very large set covering the whole range of recreational activities from arts through games to sports, with virtually everything in between. These three give an idea of the diversity: *rec.arts.sf.tv.quantum-leap*, *rec.games.xtank.programmer*, *rec.gardens.orchids*.

sci – academic and professional scientific discussion groups.

soc – most of the groups here are for discussions of different cultures, religions and social issues.

Moderation

Some newsgroups are *moderated* – someone checks articles and weeds out the irrelevant ones. Moderation is not really necessary for specialized academic or professional groups, as the quantity of articles tends to be low – and the quality high. With popular newsgroups – those on TV shows, pop stars, sports or anything to do with sex – moderation is more needed and frequently absent. These groups tend to generate huge numbers of articles – and the quality is highly variable.

11.8 Reading the news

Outlook Express offers a simple but effective routine for finding and sampling or subscribing to newsgroups.

1 Go to the news folder and click the **Newsgroups** button

or use **Tools ➡ Newsgroups** to open the panel shown opposite.

2 Type a word, or part of a word, into the **Display newsgroups which contain** box. The list is filtered to display only those groups whose names contain the given letters.

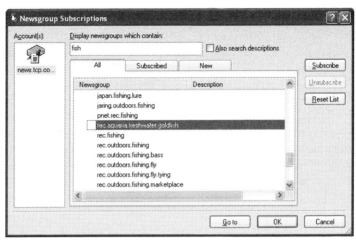

Figure 11.11 Finding newsgroups. A simple keyword search will usually produce a good selection. Collect the list of new groups from your service provider, from time to time. Initially they will be listed on the **New** tab – use **Reset list** to move them to the **All** list after you've had a chance to look through to see if any interest you.

3   When you see a group that looks interesting, select it and click **Go to**. (Or if you see a group that you know you want to read regularly, click **Subscribe**.) You will be returned to the main Outlook screen, with the selected group active.

4   If, after sampling its articles, you decide that you would like to add the group to your subscribed list, right-click on it and select **Subscribe** from the short menu.The group will be added to your news folder so you don't have to go and find it every time.

Headers and articles

A newsgroup may generate hundreds of new articles every day. Even if you are fascinated by the topic of the newsgroup, you are unlikely to want to read every article. Read the **Subjects** in the headers in the top pane to find the nature of the articles, and whether or not you want to read them.

If you want to respond to an article, either send an e-mail to the author only, or post a follow-up article to the group. In general, if the original article was a request for information, reply to the author.

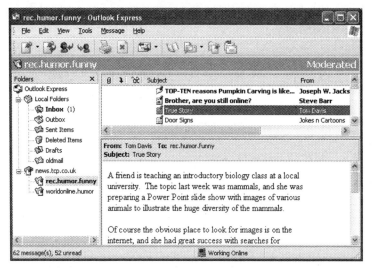

Figure 11.12 Reading the news. Select a newsgroup and download the headers, and select from there to download and read articles.

If you want to **follow up** on an article with your own contribution to the discussion, you would normally quote the relevant lines from the original article or give a brief summary of the key points that you want to pick up.

If you want to put out your own request for information, or to start a new discussion, then you **post** your article to the group.

Don't rush into posting articles. There are few things existing members find more irritating than a 'newbie' asking obvious questions or rehearsing old arguments. Spend some time 'lurking' – reading without posting – to pick up the true flavour of the group and find out what topics have been discussed recently. You should also track down the group's Frequently Asked Questions list.

Want to know more?

If you want to know more about using e-mail and the newsgroups, try *Teach Yourself the Internet*.

Summary

♦ Outlook Express handles mail and news through a set of folders. The key ones are the Inbox, where incoming mail is stored, the Outbox, where messages collect ready for sending, and the newsgroups folder.

♦ The subjects in the header lines should give you an idea of the nature of a message. You can easily reply to, or forward on, incoming mail.

♦ When composing a new message, you can use Stationery and apply formats to the text.

♦ Messages can be sent immediately, or stored for transmission later when you go online.

♦ The Options control your interaction with the system, and how and when messages are sent and read. Some options are more for newsgroups than e-mail.

♦ Use the Address Book to store the e-mail addresses of your contacts, and you will only have to type an address once!

♦ The Find People facility enables you to search some of the main people databases on the Internet.

♦ Newsgroups allow people from all over the world to share common interests and problems.

♦ There are over 50,000 newsgroups and mailing lists, covering almost every aspect of human (and alien!) life.

♦ Some groups generate huge numbers of articles – and of variable quality! You can go to a group to sample its contents, or subscribe if you intend reading regularly.

♦ Outlook Express has a good routine for finding groups, and lets you dip into them without subscribing.

♦ Don't post articles until you have got to know the nature and style of the newsgroup!

12 maintaining your system

In this chapter you will learn

- about the maintenance tools
- how to clean up and error-check your hard disks
- how to backup your files
- about System Restore
- how to format floppies

Aims of this chapter

Today's hard disks should give you years of trouble-free service. They will, however, give better service if they are maintained properly. Windows XP has tools that do all the donkey work, once you have started them off – you can even set them up so that they run automatically. Hard disks are now far more reliable than they were only a few years ago – it's unusual for them to become corrupted and lose data, even rarer to crash altogether. But these things do happen, and files can become corrupted through software errors or lost through human error. For all these reasons, it is important to protect your valuable data by backing it up regularly.

Floppy disks are more variable in quality, but reliable if treated properly. Initial formatting and checking, and careful storage is more important than regular maintenance for floppies.

12.1 The System Tools

These can all be reached from the **Start** menu, by selecting **Programs** ➡ **Accessories** ➡ **System Tools**. Open the **System Tools** menu and see what's there. You may well have a slightly different set from the one shown here.

Disk Cleanup and Disk Defragmenter can also be run from the Properties panel of any disk, or be set to run automatically with the Maintenance Wizard. Get to know these, as well-maintained disks are essential for a reliable system.

A disk – hard or floppy – is divided into *clusters*, each of which can contain all or part of one file. When a file is first written to a new disk, it will be stored in a continuous sequence of clusters, and the disk will gradually fill up from the start. If a file is edited and resaved – bigger than before – it will overwrite the original clusters then write the remainder in the next available clusters, which may well not be physically next to them on the disk. When a file is deleted, it will create a space in the middle of used area, and that later may be filled by a part of another

Figure 12.1 The **System Tools** menu.

file. Over time disks get messier, with files increasingly stored
in scattered clusters. They are still safely stored, but a file that
is held in one continuous chunk can be opened much more
quickly, simply because the system does not have to chase
around all over the disk to read it.

Disks and drives

These words are often used interchangeably, but strictly
speaking, a disk is that flat, round thing on which data is
stored, while a drive is a logical area of storage identified
by a letter (A:, C:, etc). The A: drive can have different disks
put into it. A hard disk can be partitioned to create two or
more drives.

12.2 Disk Properties

If you right-click on a drive in Windows Explorer or My Computer, and select **Properties** from the menu, the **Properties** panel
will open.

* The **General** tab shows how much used and free space you
  have on the drive.

- The **Tools** tab has buttons to start the Error-checker, Backup and Disk Defragmenter.
- The **Sharing** tab is only present if you are on a network.

Hard drives on new PCs are typically 20Gb or larger – you'll only start to run out of space if you store a lot of images, or audio or video clips.

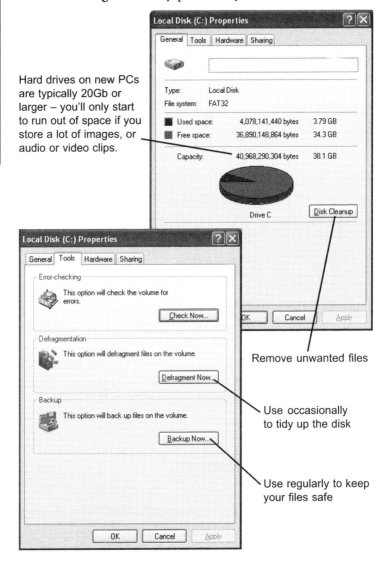

Remove unwanted files

Use occasionally to tidy up the disk

Use regularly to keep your files safe

Figure 12.2 The **General** and **Tools** tabs of the **Properties** panel for a C: drive.

12.3 Disk Cleanup

This is the simplest of the system tools, and one that should be run fairly regularly to free up space. It removes temporary and other unwanted files from the hard disk.

When you start Disk Cleanup, the first job is to select the drive – normally C:. You then select the sets of files to delete.

* **Temporary Internet Files** – don't remove these if you want to be able to revisit pages without having to go online again.

* **Downloaded Program Files** refer to Java or ActiveX applets (small programs) that you met on Web pages, and which had to be stored on your disk so that the programs could be run.

* **Recycle Bin** – this just saves you having to empty the Bin as a separate operation.

* **Temporary files** refers to those created by applications – typically automatic backups and print files. They are normally cleaned up when the application is closed, but may

Figure 12.3 Disk Cleanup. On the **More Options** tab you can remove unwanted Windows components or programs.

be left behind especially if it ends with a crash. Disk Cleanup will not touch new files, which the application may still be using.

After you have made your selection and clicked **OK**, you will be prompted to confirm the deletions – they are irreversible – before the cleanup starts.

12.4 Error-checking

In earlier versions of Windows, the error-checking routine was not that simple to run, but offered quite good control of what to do about any errors that it found. The new error checker is very simple to run, with only two options at the start, and nothing for you to do once it's running. In fact, once it's running you can't do anything at all on the PC.

◆ If no option is set, the routine simply checks that the files are stored safely. You can set one or other of these options.

◆ With **Automatically fix file system errors** on, the routine will try to solve any problems that it meets – and as it will almost certainly do this better than you or me, I'd leave it to it!

◆ The **Scan for and attempt recovery of bad sectors** will fix file system errors and also test the surface of the disk, to make sure that files can be stored safely, and rebuild it if necessary.

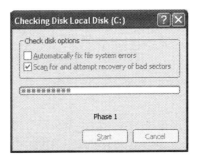

Figure 12.4 Error-checking in progress. There is very little to see except the progress bar. Phase 1 is quite fast; Phase 2 takes ages on a big disk – go and have a coffee while it works.

12.5 Disk Defragmenter

We noted earlier that the storage space on a disk is divided into clusters, and that a file may occupy any number of clusters, each linked to the next. On a new, clean disk, each file will normally be written in a set of clusters that are physically continuous on the disk. Over time, as the disk fills up, and as files are written, rewritten (larger or smaller) and deleted, it gradually becomes more difficult to store files in adjacent clusters – the disk is becoming *fragmented*. The files are still safe, but they cannot be read as quickly if the reading heads have to hop all over the disk.

Disk Defragmenter reorganizes the physical storage of files on the disk, pulling together the data from scattered clusters. Though it improves performance, the gains are in the order of a few seconds for starting a program or loading a data file, and it is a very slow job – allow an hour on a 20Gb disk. It is only worth doing regularly if your disk is getting full – so that new files are being stored in a limited area – or if you have a high turnover of files from working on large databases or reports, or from installing and removing demos, shareware and other programs.

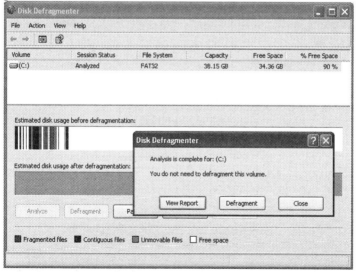

Figure 12.5 Always analyse first. You do not want to run a defragment unless you have to – it takes too long!

12.6 Backup

If an application's program files become corrupted or accidentally deleted, it is a nuisance but not a major problem as you
can simply reinstall the application from the original disks.
Data files are a different matter. How much is your data worth
to you? How long would it take you to rewrite that report,
redraw that picture or re-enter the last six months' accounts if
they were lost? Individual files can be copied onto floppies for
safekeeping, but if you have more than one or two it is simpler
to use Backup. A backup job is easily set up, doesn't take long
to run and will more than pay for itself in time and trouble the
first time that you need it!

Backup media

Backups can be done on floppy disks, and this is fine for home
use or in a small business where there's not a lot to backup –
with compression, over 2Mb of data will fit on one disk. If you
intend to backup large quantities of data regularly, invest £100
or so in a tape drive or an IOmega removable hard disk system
– it will be far easier than struggling with a pile of floppies.

Whatever you save onto must be removable. You must be able
to store the backup away from the machine – in a fireproof
safe or a different building if you want real security.

The Backup or Restore Wizard

When you start the wizard, you will be asked if you want to
back up files or restore them from a backup. Select *backup*.

1 At the first stage, if you want a full backup – of everything on
   your system – select **All information on this computer**. This is
   not a viable option if you are backing up on floppy disks!

2 If you opt to back up selected files and folders, you will be
   given an Explorer-style display. Click the ⊞ icons to open
   out the folders as necessary.

   Simply tick a folder if you want to back up everything in it.

   To select items within a folder, click on its name to open it,
   then tick individual items.

3 Select the medium (tape, disk, etc.) and drive if saving to
   disk, and give your backup job a name – this should describe the file selection and the date.

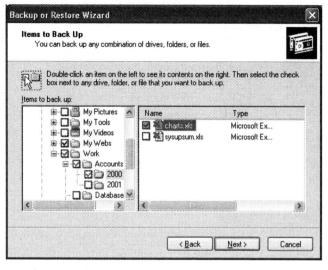

Figure 12.6 Selecting files to back up. If you select a folder, all its contents are selected – click on the folder name to list its contents if you only want to back up selected files, then clear the checkboxes for those that you do not want to back up.

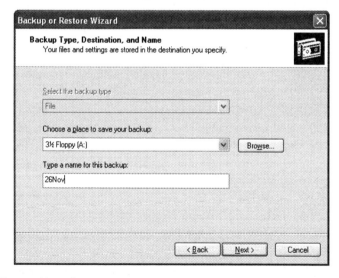

Figure 12.7 Give the backup a name that will identify it clearly.

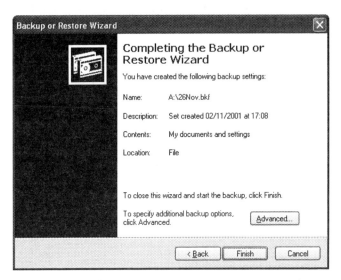

Figure 12.8 The Backup summary panel. Click Advanced if you need to set more options.

4 At the next, and usually final, stage, you will see a summary of the backup settings. If everything is OK, click **Finish**. If you are backing up a lot of data onto floppies, you should now sit ready to change the disks on request.

Advanced Backup settings

The **Advanced** button on the summary panel will let you set more options.

The **Type of Backup** can be:

- **Normal**, which copies all the selected files and marks them as backed up;

- **Copy**, which copies all the selected files, but without marking them as backed up;

- **Incremental** saves only those changed since last the Normal backup;

- **Differential** also saves only changed files, but without marking them as backed up;

- **Daily** saves only files created on the current day.

At the following stages you can specify the nature, placing and scheduling of the backup. If you are using a backup tape or other high capacity media, it makes sense to run the backup after you have finished work.

Restoring files

With any luck this will never be necessary!

1 Run **Backup**, and select **Restore** at the opening panel.

2 Insert the disk or tape with the backup into its drive.

3 Select the backup file.

4 Open the folders as necessary until you can see the files and folders that you want to restore. Tick to select them.

5 Click **Next** – that's it.

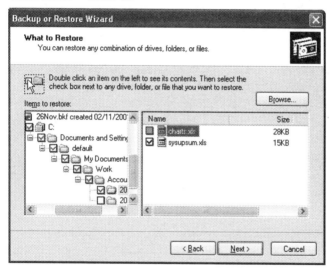

Figure 12.9 Restoring a file from a backup – not difficult, and far, far easier than trying to recreate it from scratch!

12.7 System Restore

With any luck you'll never need this, but it's good to know that it is there. Windows automatically stores a backup copy of important system files, known as system restore points, at regular intervals. If these files become corrupted for any reason, e.g. 'user error', new software installation problems or hardware failure, System Restore will get your system running again.

To restore your system:

1 Go to the **System Tools** menu and select **System Restore**.

2 At the first stage, select **Restore my computer...**

3 At the next panel, pick the most recent checkpoint when you know that the system was running properly.

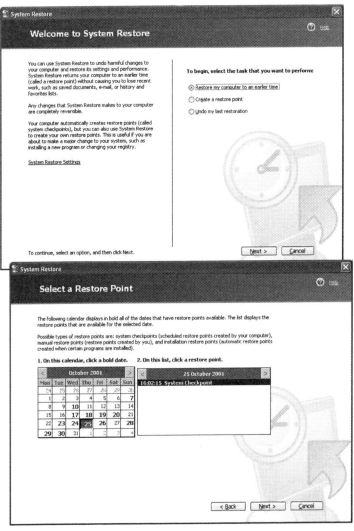

Figure 12.10 Using **System Restore**.

Creating a restore point

A Windows XP computer is robust, and modern software and hardware is normally reliable and thoroughly tested, but things do go wrong. Before you do anything which might upset the system, such as installing new kit or making any other major changes, create a restore point. It takes only a few minutes and could save you endless hours of pain!

1 Start **System Restore** and select **Create a restore point**.

2 Type in a description to help you identify it – the point will have the date and time added, so this is not too crucial.

3 Click **Next** to start the process.

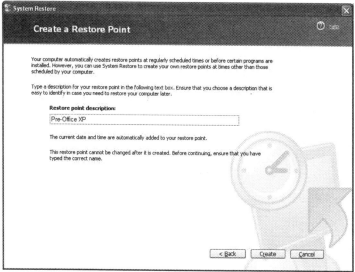

Figure 12.11 Creating a restore point – insure against the unforeseen!

12.8 Floppy disks

These are mainly used for backups and for copying files from one PC to another. Before use they will need formatting – unless you have bought them ready-formatted.

1 Place an unformatted disk in the floppy drive.

2 Right-click on the **A:** icon in My Computer or Explorer and select **Format…** from the menu.

3 At the Format dialog box, in **Format Type**, select *Full*. A *Quick* format will erase files from a formatted disk; *Copy system files* is used to create a startup disk.

4 Type a **Label** if wanted – the paper label is more use for identifying floppies.

5 Click **Start**.

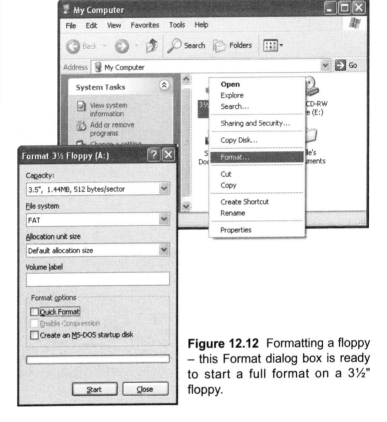

Figure 12.12 Formatting a floppy – this Format dialog box is ready to start a full format on a 3½" floppy.

Floppy care

Floppies are quite robust, but their files can be corrupted if exposed to heat or magnetism. Keep them away from radiators, magnets, heavy machinery and electricity cables.

Formatting the C: drive

Don't do it! Formatting destroys all the data on a disk. *Do not format the C: drive!* The option is there, but it should only ever be used as a last-ditch attempt to recover something from the ruins of a major virus attack or other total failure – and only ever with professional advice. Otherwise, *don't do it!*

Summary

◆ Hard disks need regular maintenance to keep them in good condition. Windows XP provides tools for this.

◆ The maintenance utilities can be started from the System Tools menu, or from the Tools tab of a disk's Properties panel.

◆ Disk Cleanup will remove temporary and unwanted files.

◆ Use Error-checking regularly to ensure that your files and folders are intact and correctly stored.

◆ Disk Defragmenter will reorganize the disk so that files are stored in continuous sequences for faster reading.

◆ Backup will help you to keep organized copies of your files. Use it regularly. You may never need it, but if you do, you'll be glad that your backups are there!

◆ System Restore can help to recover the system from calamity.

◆ Floppies must be formatted before use.

printers

In this chapter you will learn

- how to install a new printer
- about printer properties
- how to set printing options
- how to manage the print queue
- how to print a document from My Computer

Aims of this chapter

Many printers are 'plug and play' – just connect them, and Windows XP will configure the system so that they can be used. Sometimes you need to install the drivers – the programs that convert the PC's formatting codes into ones for the printer – and controlling software. Here we look at how to manage printers and how to install those that aren't plug and play.

13.1 Adding a new printer

If your printer dates from before XP's release in Autumn 2001, the drivers available in Windows XP will probably be newer than those supplied with the printer. If it is more recent, dig out its installation disk.

Click to start the wizard

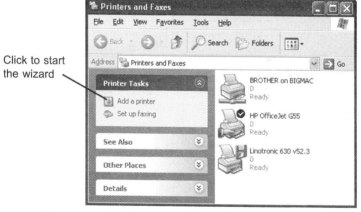

This PC has several printers – the OfficeJet is the default (shown by ⊘); the Brother is on the network.

The **Add Printer Wizard** makes installation simple.

1 Open the **Printers** folder, from the **Start** menu.

2 Click **Add a printer** to run the wizard.

3 At the first screen, select *Local printer*, if it is attached to your PC, or *Network printer* if you access it through your

office Local Area Network. Turn off the *Automatically detect and install option* – if it was going to work, it would have done so already!

4 For a local printer, you need to choose the port – normally LPT1. If you have a (rare) serial printer, use a COM port – COM4 may be free.

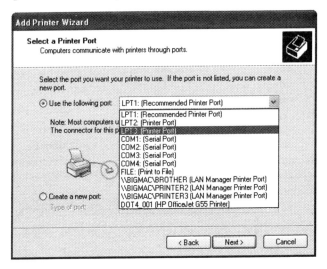

Figure 13.1 Selecting a port for the printer. The COM ports are normally used to connect the mouse and modem. Select FILE if you are outputting files for remote printing, e.g. at a commercial printers.

5 For a network printer, browse the network to find the printer you want to use.

6 If you are using one of the Windows XP drivers, select the **Manufacturer** from the list, then the **Printer** model. If you are using the drivers supplied with the printer, click **Have Disk**, then select the model from the list that is drawn from the disk.

7 You may want to edit the full manufacturer/model name into something shorter to label the icon in the Printers folder.

8 If you have more than one printer, one is set as the *default* – the one to use unless you specify otherwise when you start printing.

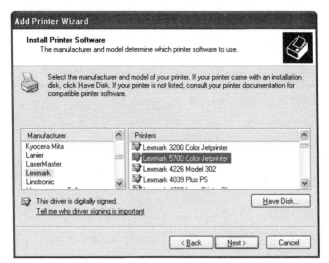

Figure 13.2 You should find software for virtually all printers in use when Windows XP was developed. If a **Windows Update** button appears, newer drivers may be available online for this printer. With a newer one, use its own software – click **Have Disk**.

◆ If you are on a network, and have installed a local printer, you will be asked if you want to share it. If you do, give it a name.

9 At the final stage, accept the offer of a test print – it's as well to check! Once you click **Finish**, the Wizard will load the driver from the disk and install it in your system.

13.2 Printer Properties

Before you use the printer, check its properties. If nothing else, you may well need to change the paper size, as it is often set to the US 'Letter' (216 × 279mm). The standard UK paper size is A4 (210 × 297mm).

Right-click on the new icon in the Printers folder and select **Properties**. Different printers have different Properties panels, but you should find:

◆ A **General** tab, where you can type a comment. This is mainly useful on a network, to tell others of any special requirements that you or the printer have.

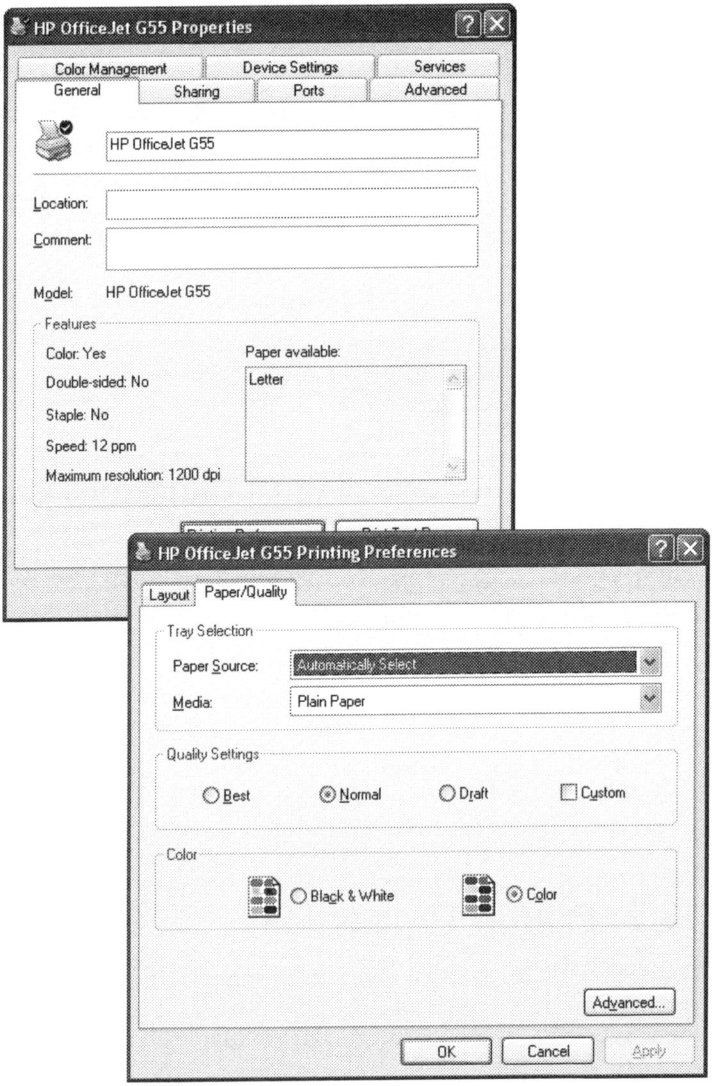

Figure 13.3 The **Properties** and **Preferences** panels for a printer. Take time to explore yours to see what options are available, and what defaults have been set – not all may make sense at first! Remember that these are only the default settings, and that they can be changed, from within an application, before printing a document.

- An **Advanced** tab, where you can select a new driver if needed. The **Spool** settings determine whether the file is sent directly from the application to the printer, or through a temporary memory buffer. Spooling frees up applications, as they can generally send data out faster than the printer can handle it.

- A **Printing Defaults** or **Preferences** button, which leads to a dialog box where you can set the paper size. The other options here are best left at their defaults, though you may want to change them before printing specific documents.

- A **Device Settings** panel. Check the **Memory** (normally only with laser printers). If you have added extra memory – a good idea if you print pages with lots of graphics – tell Windows.

13.3 Printing from applications

The Print routines in applications are all much the same. There will usually be a 🖨 toolbar button, and clicking on this will send the document to the printer using its current settings –

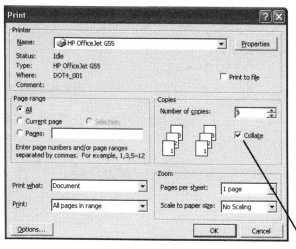

With multiple copies, turning **Collate** on, makes printing take longer, but you won't have to sort a pile of paper afterwards

Figure 13.4 The Print dialog box from Word. Other applications have different options, but **Page range** and **Copies** are common to all.

whatever they are. The first time that you print something, it is best to start by selecting **Print** from the **File** menu. This will open a dialog box where you can define the settings – the key ones are which pages to print and how many copies.

If you need to change the layout, print quality or other printer settings, clicking the **Properties** button will open the printer's properties panel – this may look slightly different from the panel opened from the Printers folder, but gives you access to the same settings.

13.4 Controlling the print queue

Unless you are exceptionally disorganized or have very unreliable hardware, most of your printing will run smoothly. But things go wrong even at the most organized desk…

When a document is sent for printing, it goes first to the print queue. If it is the only print job, it is then processed directly. If not, it will sit in the queue and wait its turn. As long as a document is still in the queue, you can do something about it – but if it is just one short, simple document, it will almost certainly be through the queue before you can get to it.

- If you discover a late error, so that printing is just a waste of paper, a job can be cancelled.

- If you have sent a series of documents in succession, you can change the order in which they are printed.

When the printer is active, you will see ![icon] on the right of the Taskbar. Click on it to open the printer's folder, where the queue is stored.

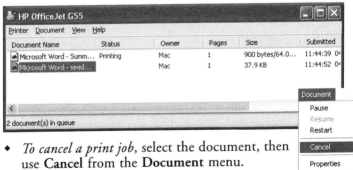

- *To cancel a print job*, select the document, then use **Cancel** from the **Document** menu.

- *To cancel all the queued jobs,* use **Cancel All Documents** from the **Printer** menu.

  Don't just turn off! Turning off the printer is not a good way to stop a print job. If the document is partially printed or waiting in the queue it will start to print again as soon as the printer is turned back on – and if partially printed, will be probably be garbled. You must clear the queue to get rid of a print job.

- *To change the order of printing,* select a document and drag it up or down the queue as required – this only works with those documents that are not already being spooled or printed.

13.5 Printing from file

You can print a document from Windows Explorer or My Computer, as long as you have an application which can handle it. Windows will open the application, print the document, then close the application for you.

Figure 13.5 You can print a document directly from file.

To send the document to the default printer:

* Select the file and click **Print this file** in the **File and Folder Tasks** list.

Or

* If you have the Folder list open, right-click on the file and select **Print** from the short menu.

Summary

* To install a new printer, use the Add Printer Wizard in the Printers folder. Windows XP has drivers for almost every known printer model.

* Check the printer's Properties panel before use, to make sure that the default settings – especially the paper size – are suitable.

* When printing from an application, you can usually set the page range and number of copies. If required, the printer Properties can be adjusted before printing.

* Documents are taken to the print queue before output. By opening the queue you can cancel a print job or change the order in which they are printed.

* A document can be printed from Windows Explorer or My Computer.

14

the accessories

In this chapter you will learn

- about some of the accessories – WordPad, Character Map, Paint, the Scanner and Camera Wizard, Calculator, Media Player and Movie Maker
- how to set up a home network

Aims of this chapter

The Windows XP package includes a host of accessories – some very useful, others just for fun. In this chapter we will be looking at a selection of these. Even if you never use any of these accessories in earnest, it is worth experimenting with them, as the skills and knowledge that you learn here can be applied to other Windows applications.

14.1 WordPad

Don't underrate WordPad just because it's free. It has all the facilities that you would have found in the top-flight software of just a few years ago, and compares well with today's commercial packages. It's fine for writing letters, essays, reports, source code for computer programs and anything else where you want to be able to edit text efficiently, formatting it with fonts, styles and colours, and perhaps incorporating graphics or other files.

* When entering text, just keep typing when you reach the edge of the page – the text will be wrapped round to the next line. Only press the **Enter** key at the end of a paragraph.

* Existing text can be selected, with the normal techniques, then moved, deleted or formatted.

* Most formatting can be done through the toolbar. Select the text, then pick a font or size from the drop-down lists, or click the Ⓑ bold, Ⓘ italic, ⓤ underline, 🎨 colour or other buttons.

* The ≡ left, ≡ centre and ≡ right alignment buttons determine how the text lines up with the edges of the paper.

* The ⦂≡ bullets button indents text from the left, with a blob at the start of each paragraph.

* Alignment and bullet formats apply to whole paragraphs. You do not need to select the whole paragraph – if the cursor is within it, or part of its text is selected, the paragraph will be formatted.

Standard toolbar – with the main filing and editing tools

Formatting toolbar   Ruler

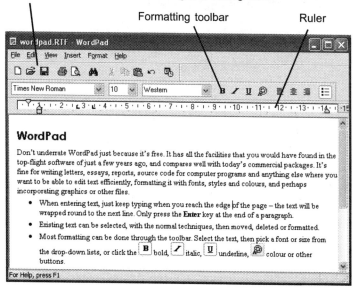

Figure 14.1 WordPad, being used to create the text for these pages!

Indents and tabs

These are best set from the ruler. Select the text where new indents or tabs are required then drag the icons to set the indent; click to set a tab point.

Left margin   Right margin
  First line indent   Right indent

Tab

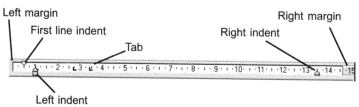

Left indent

Full font formatting

Though you can set almost all font options from the toolbar buttons, you get better control through the **Font** panel – open it with **Format ➜ Font**. Here you can set all aspects of the selected text, and preview the effects of your choices. Watch the **Sample** text as you change the settings.

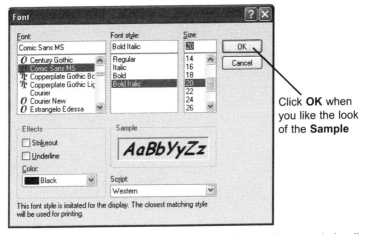

Click **OK** when
you like the look
of the **Sample**

Figure 14.2 The **Font** dialog box. You'll find similar panels in all
applications that use fonts

Page Setup

The **Page Setup** panel, opened from the **File** menu option,
controls the basic size and layout of the page – for all pages in
the document.

This is Portrait
Orientation.

WordPad.
Measurements here
are in centimetres,
but can be changed
on the **Options**
panel that opens
from the **View** menu.

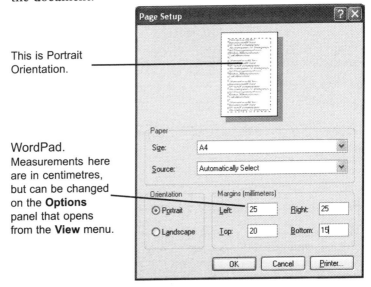

Figure 14.3 The **Page Setup** panel in

- The **Paper Size** and **Source** settings rarely need changing – if you've set your printer properties correctly. If you are printing on card or special paper, change the **Source** to *Manual*, if the option is available.

- In the **Orientation** area, *Portrait* is the normal way up; use *Landscape* if you want to print with the paper sideways.

- The **Margins** set the overall limits to the printable area. You can use the indents to reduce the width of text within the margins, but you cannot extend out beyond them.

- Click the **Printer** button to reach its **Properties** panel to change any settings at that level – you might, for example, want to switch to a lower resolution for printing a draft copy, or a higher resolution for the final output. (At low resolution, the printer will work faster and use less ink or toner.)

Graphics and other objects

WordPad is not limited to text only. Pictures, graphs, spreadsheets, audio and video clips – in fact just about any object that can be produced by any Windows application – can be incorporated into a WordPad document. The technique is much the same for any object.

1 Open the **Insert** menu and select **Object**...

2 If the object does not yet exist, select the **Object Type** and click **OK**. The appropriate application will open. When you have created the object, save it if you want to keep a separate copy for future use, then select the new **Exit & Return to Document** option from the **File** menu.

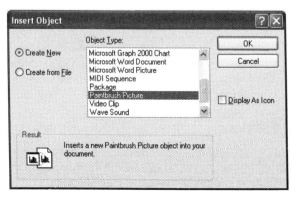

3   If you want to use an existing object, select **Create from File**, and browse through your folders to locate it.

4   Back in WordPad, you can move or resize the object. Select it – it will be outlined with handles at the corners and mid-edges.

Point to a handle to get the double-headed arrow then drag in or out as required. The position of the object across the page can be set by using the alignment buttons.

> You can't do fancy layouts with WordPad. An image can sit by itself, separate from the text above and below, or can be embedded in a single line. That's it.

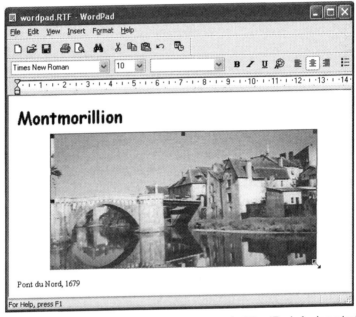

Figure 14.4 Adjusting the size of an image in WordPad. An inserted object can be edited by double-clicking on it – this opens the source application. Use **Exit & Return** when you have finished editing.

Print Preview

Like almost all applications, WordPad has a Print Preview facility. Working on screen, it can be difficult to tell how a document will look on paper – you may not be able to see the full width of the page and you certainly won't be able to see the full height. Use the Preview to get a better idea of the printed output, before you commit it to paper. Are your images or headings large enough to make the impact that you want? Do you get awkward breaks in the text at the ends of pages? If you are happy with the look of your document, you can print from here by clicking the **Print** button, otherwise, click **Close** to return to WordPad for further tweaking.

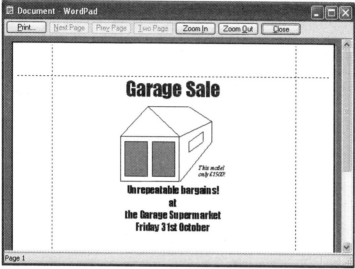

Figure 14.5 Using the Page preview facility to check the overall layout of a page. You can print from here, or close to return to editing.

Saving and opening files

In WordPad as in all applications you should save early and save often! Don't wait until you have finished writing that eight-page report before you save it. Applications can crash, hardware can fail, plugs get knocked out and we all make mistakes!

The first save may take a few moments, but later saves are done at the click of a button.

To save a file for the first time:

1 Open the **File** menu and select **Save As...**
2 At the dialog box, select the folder.

3 Change the default 'Document' in the filename to something that will remind you what it is about.

4 RTF (Rich Text Format) is the standard WordPad format – it can be read by many applications. If you want to save in a different format, pick one from the **Save as type** drop-down list.

5 Click **Save**.

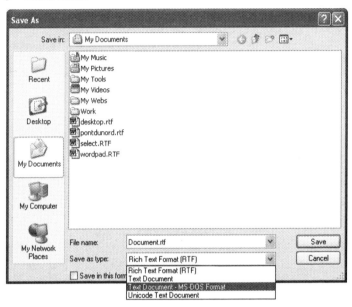

Figure 14.6 The **Save** dialog box in WordPad.

To resave the current document, click ▣ – that's it!

When you close the document, or exit from WordPad, if you have not saved the document in its final state, you will be prompted to do so.

Next time that you want to work on the document, open it from the **File** menu. Either:

• Select **Open** and then browse for the file – the dialog box is used in almost exactly the same way as the Save dialog box.

• If it is one of the files that you have used most recently, it will be listed at the bottom of the **File** menu. Just select it from here.

14.2 Character Map

You will find **Character Map** on the **System Tools** menu – don't ask me why! It's a useful tool and one that I like to have close to hand. It allows you to see the characters available in any font, and to copy individual characters from there into a document.

1   Pick a font from the drop-down list – Symbol, Webdings and Wingdings are the main fonts for decorative characters, and you will find foreign letters and mathematical symbols in most other fonts.

2   Click on the character for an enlargement – if you hold down the left button and move across the characters, enlargements will appear as you go.

3   To copy characters into a document, click **Select** – the current one will be added to the **Characters to copy** display – then click **Copy** when you have all you want. Return to your document and use **Edit ➡ Paste** – the character(s) will be copied in, formatted to the chosen font.

Click or drag across the display to see an enlargement

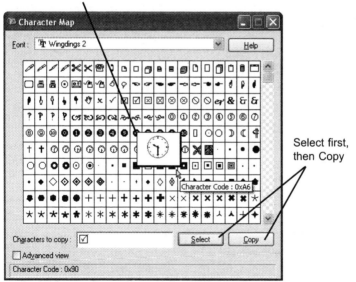

Select first, then Copy

Figure 14.7 Character Map.

14.3 Paint

Graphics software falls into two broad groups. The first type works with objects – lines, circles, text boxes, etc. – that remain separate, and can be moved, deleted, recoloured and otherwise changed at any point. Word's Drawing facility works this way.

In the second type, which includes Paint, the image is produced by applying colour to a background – with each new line overwriting anything that may be beneath. Using these is very like real painting. You may be able to wipe out a mistake while the paint is still wet, but as soon as it has dried it is fixed on the canvas. (Paint allows you to undo the last move.) I use Paint regularly – it's ideal for trimming and tidying screenshots for books, though I don't expect many of you will want it for this purpose. Though it can be used to produce intricate images, these can be created more successfully on a computer art package, with a full set of shading, shaping and manipulating tools. Paint is probably best used to draw simple diagrams, or as a children's toy, or to get an idea of how this type of graphics software works.

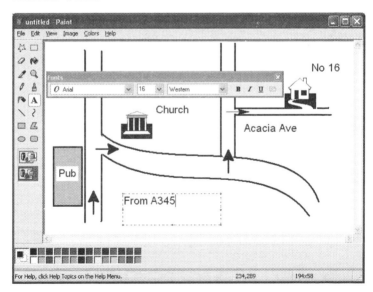

Figure 14.8 Using Paint to create a diagram. The **Text toolbar** gives you the full range of fonts and the main style effects.

The Toolbox

There is a simple but adequate set of tools. A little experimentation will show how they all work.

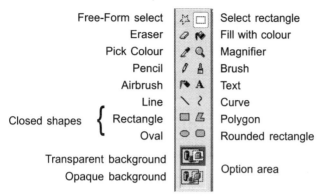

Free-Form select	Select rectangle
Eraser	Fill with colour
Pick Colour	Magnifier
Pencil	Brush
Airbrush	Text
Line	Curve
Closed shapes { Rectangle	Polygon
Oval	Rounded rectangle
Transparent background	
Opaque background	Option area

Most of them have options that can be set in the area below the toolbar.

◆ When you select an area (or paste an image from file or the Clipboard) the background can be transparent or opaque.

◆ You can set the size of the Eraser, Brush, Airbrush, Line and Curve. N.B. the Line thickness applies to the closed shapes.

◆ The Magnifier is 4× by default, but can be 2×, 6× or 8×.

◆ The Pencil is only ever 1 pixel wide.

◆ Closed shapes can be outline or fill only, or both.

The Curve is probably the trickiest of the tools to use. The line can have one or two curves to it.

1 Draw a line between the points where the curve will start and end.

2 Drag to create the first curve – exaggerate the curve as it will normally be reduced at the next stage.

3 If the line is to have a second curve, drag it out now – as long as the mouse button is down, the line will flex to follow the cursor.

4 For a simple curve, just click at the end of the line.

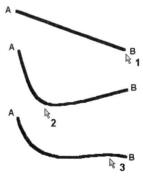

Undo it!

If you go wrong any time – and you will with the Curve – use **Edit ➡Undo**. This removes the effect of the last action.

Working with selected areas

The rectangular and free-form selectors can be used to select an area of the screen. Once selected, an area can be:

◆ Deleted – use this for removing mistakes and excess bits.

◆ Copied – handy for creating repeating patterns.

◆ Saved as a file – use **Edit ➡Copy To...** and give a filename.

◆ Dragged elsewhere on screen.

◆ Flipped (mirrored) horizontally or vertically, or rotated in 90° increments – use **Image ➡Flip/Rotate** for these effects.

◆ Stretched – to enlarge, shrink or distort, or skewed, either horizontally or vertically – use **Image ➡Stretch/Skew**.

Colours

The colour palette is used in almost the same way in all Windows programs. You can select a colour from the basic set – use the left button for the foreground colour and the right button for the background – or you can mix your own colours.

Double-click on a colour in the **Color Box** or use **Colors ➡ Edit Colors** to open the **Edit Colors** panel. Initially only the **Basic colors** will be visible. Click **Define Custom Colors** to open the full panel.

To define a new colour, drag the cross-hair cursor in the main square to set the Red/Green/Blue balance, and move the arrow up or down the left scale to set the light/dark level. Colours can also be set by typing in values, but note that you are mixing light, not paint. Red and green make yellow; red, green and blue make grey/white; the more you use, the lighter the colour.

When you have the colour you want, click **Add to Custom Colors**. The new colour will replace the one currently selected in the Color Box on the main screen.

Set the Red/Green/Blue balance

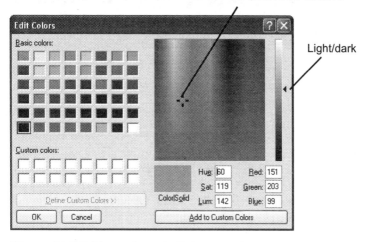

Light/dark

Figure 14.9 Editing colours in Paint.

Filing

Saving and opening files is the same here as in WordPad. You can also use **Edit ➡ Copy To...** to save part of an image and **Edit ➡ Paste From...** to open a file so that you can combine its image with the existing picture. The image will come in as a selected area, which can be positioned wherever required. Set the background to transparent to merge the two images, or to opaque for the new file to overlay the old image.

Screenshots

If you press the **Prt Sc** (Print Screen) key, the whole screen display will be copied into the Clipboard. If you press **Alt + Prt Sc** then only the active window will be copied into the Clipboard. The image can then be pasted into Paint, or any other graphics program, and saved from there. That's how the screenshots were produced for this book.

14.4 Scanner and Camera Wizard

You can use this to take images in from a scanner or a digital camera and store them in a folder. If you want to take an image directly into a graphics program, for editing, then it is normally simpler to start from within that program – look for **From Scanner or Camera** or **Acquire Image** or similar command on the **File** menu.

The wizard first calls up the control panel for the scanner. Here you can define the picture type and the area to be scanned – use the preview to define the area, unless you want to scan a full page. At the next stage, you specify the filename, its format and the folder in which to store it. After the picture has been captured, you will be given the option of also publishing the images on your Web site or ordering printed copies from an online photo printer.

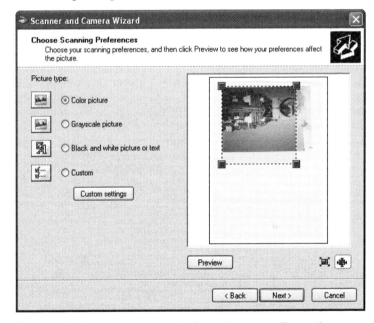

Figure 14.10 A scanner control panel – you will see the same panel whether you start your scanner from within Paint or other graphics software. If you are doing a high resolution scan, define the area tightly to keep the file size and scanning time down as far as possible.

14.5 Calculator

Pack away that pocket calculator. You don't need it on your desk now that you have one on your Desktop!

The Calculator can work in two modes – Standard or Scientific – use the View menu options to switch between them.

In either mode, use the Calculator in the same way that you would a hand-held one. Enter the numbers, arithmetic operators and functions either by clicking on the screen keys, or from your keyboard. (You can still use the keyboard when in the Scientific mode as there are keyboard shortcuts for the extra buttons – look in the Help file for the list of 'keyboard equivalents of calculator buttons'.)

It has the same limitations as a pocket calculator – you can only store one value in memory at a time (**MS** to store it, **M+** to add to the value in memory, **MR** to recall it and **MC** to clear it); and you cannot print your results (though you can copy the result into another document). If you want more than this, use a spreadsheet!

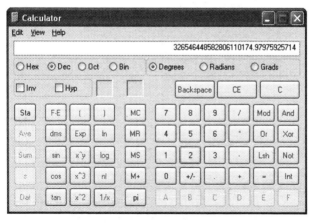

Figure 14.11 The Calculator in Scientific mode. In either mode, it works to 32-digit accuracy – is that close enough for you?

14.6 Media Player

Media Player is a multi-purpose audio/video player. It can play sound files in MIDI and in the native Windows format, WAVE – as well as audio CDs – or video in the standard Video for Windows (AVI), Media Audio/Video (WMA and ASF) or the many ActiveMovie formats.

CD Audio

Want some music while you work? Let Media Player play a CD for you.

1 Put the CD into the drive and wait for a moment for Media Player to start up and to read in the track information.

◆ The CD will play the tracks in their playlist sequence – initially this will be the standard order.

2 To change the order of tracks, click on one to select it, then drag up or down.

3 To skip over tracks, select them, then right-click and choose **Disable** from the shortcut menu.

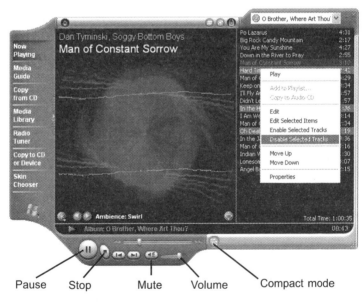

Figure 14.12 Media Player, showing the playlist for an audio CD.

It's worth taking time over this, as any choices or other informa-tion that you enter here are recorded by Windows in a file (on the hard disk – it can't write to the CD) and will be reused next time the same CD is loaded.

Once the playlist is set up and the CD is playing, you can switch into compact mode. This doesn't just occupy less screen space, it also has some great 'skins'. How about this one for really hi-tech hi-fi! (Well, maybe.)

Return to Full mode

This has the default 'visualization' running in it. If you don't like it – and I do – there are plenty of alternatives. Open the **View** menu, point to **Visualization**, select a set then pick from there. The names are not terribly helpful – you'll have to watch them to make a proper choice.

Radio

This offers another way to get radio over the Internet (see page 173). There are a dozen pre-set stations, catering to a range of

Figure 14.13 Listening to Jazz FM, while looking to see what stations offer classical music – there are dozens, how do I choose one?!

tastes, or you can use the Station Finder facility to pick from the hundreds of stations that are now broadcasting. You will find, when choosing a station, that Internet Explorer will normally open to show you the station's Web site. This can be closed down, if not wanted, to save screen space and speed up download of the broadcast.

Obviously, if you are paying for your phone time when you are online, this is not an efficient way to listen to the radio!

Video

Newer, faster hardware and more efficient software has significantly improved the quality of videos on PC, but they are still small and jerky – or run them in full-screen mode and they are large and blocky and jerky!

The main sources of videos are multimedia packages, where Media Player can be called up automatically to play the clips, demos and samples on CDs, and – most of all – the Internet.

There are three main ways in which you will get video from the Internet:

◆ Clips for downloading – the new high-compression formats have brought a better balance between download time and playing time. 1Mb of video gives you around 90 seconds of playing time, and will take up to 10 minutes to download – and you must have the whole file on your disk before you can start to play it.

◆ Streaming video in TV and webcam broadcasts and, increasingly, in movie and pop video clips. Here the videos are played as they download. The images are jerkier, but at least you don't have to wait to see whether they are worth watching at all.

◆ Home movies e-mailed to you by relatives, who also have Windows XP and have been playing with its Movie Maker.

Portable Device

CD audio tracks and files, from the Internet or elsewhere, in MP3, WAV, WMA or ASF formats can be copied through Media Player onto your MP3 player or other portable device.

14.7 Movie Maker

You can use this to edit digital video, taking images in directly from your camera. The video is split into clips, which can then be split further or trimmed and set into a new sequence. You can merge in other video clips, or add still pictures, for titles and credits, or a voice-over or background music. If you have the time and the skill, you can produce some good movies with this neat editing suite.

The Movie Maker format takes around 10Kb for each second of playing time. This means that video files are not small, though they are very much more compact than the ones produced by older formats, and sharing them with distant friends and relatives via the Internet is now quite feasible.

There are two ways to do it:

• Send the movie by e-mail. Files are increased in size by 50% when attached to a message (it's to do with the way that

Figure 14.14 Playing with the sample file in Movie Maker. I don't think I've got a future in the movies, but you may have!

data is transferred through the mail system), but you can normally download e-mail at 3Kb or more per second.

◆ Upload the file to your web site, and send the URL to people. There are two catches to this: you have to have at least a basic grasp of putting home pages together, and download times from the Web are typically less than 2Kb per second.

What it boils down to is that it is going to take your distant friends and relatives around one minute to download 100Kb of video, which will play for 10 seconds. That 10 minute video of the little one's birthday party will take over an hour to get, and as for the school's Christmas panto...

14.8 Home networking

Setting up even a small network used to be a chore. Windows 95 introduced some tools which simplified it, but it was still not a job for the non-technical. The **Network Set up Wizard** transforms the business. It is so easy to use – with two provisos.

◆ Networking is quite straightforward as long as you are simply connecting Windows XP PCs together. In theory, you can also connect to older Windows 95 or 98 PCs, but you are likely to run into compatibility problems. If you want to share an Internet connection, the PC with the modem must be an XP PC.

◆ You still have to open the PCs' boxes and install the network cards, and their software, then cable them together.

To start the **Network Set up Wizard**, select the *Set up a network* option in the **New Connection Wizard** or in the **Network Connections** folder.

The Wizard takes care of setting up the Windows' networking software. All you need to do is tell it a few things about your system, and decide what to call the PCs. Initially only the Shared Documents folder in each PC will be shared across the nework; other folders can be shared later by opening their Properties panel and turning on sharing.

Once the network is in place, you can then run the **Connect to the Internet** routine in the New Connection Wizard on the PC that does *not* have the modem. Choose to set up the connection manually and through a LAN (Local Area Network).

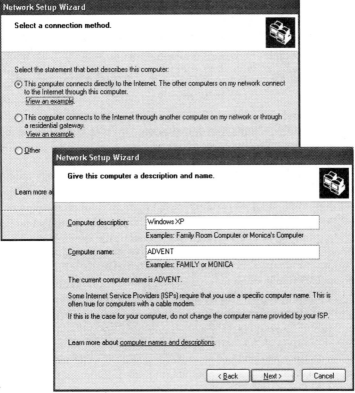

Figure 14.15 Working through the Home Networking Wizard. If the PC has an Internet connection, the Wizard will ask for details. You can adjust how you share folders and printers at any time.

Work through the stages of the Wizard, accepting the defaults where they are offered, and letting the Wizard sort out all the technical details.

The connection is fully shared. Not only can all the networked machines use the connection, they can use it at the same time.

ISPs and connection sharing

Internet connection sharing may not work with some ISPs. If you have problems, check that they can handle it.

Summary

* The techniques that you learn using the accessories can be applied to other Windows applications.

* WordPad has enough formatting and layout facilities to cope with many word-processing jobs.

* Character Map will let you examine the characters in any font. Characters can be copied from here and pasted into documents.

* Paint is a simple graphics program that can be used for creating diagrams, fun pictures and for editing and saving screenshots.

* You can use the Scanner and Camera Wizard to take in images and store them in folders.

* Calculator will do the job of a simple or a scientific pocket calculator.

* Media Player can play audio CDs, and audio and video files in most formats.

* You can produce your own movies with Movie Maker.

* The Network Setup Wizard makes it very simple to network your PCs together, and with Internet Connection sharing, they can all get online through the same modem.

taking it further

I hope that this *Teach Yourself* has helped you to get to grips with Windows XP, and that you are now ready to take your use of Windows further. The best way to gain confidence with Windows is to play with it, and the best way to master Windows is to use it.

Play with Windows! Play the games – it's good for your eye–hand coordination and the development of your mouse and keyboard skills. Play with the display properties – it will encourage you to explore the system, give you practice in using dialog boxes and setting options, and you should finish up with a screen that looks just the way you want it. Play with the filing system – but play carefully! Make some 'toys' – test files that you can lose without worrying about them.

Use Windows! You can do lots without even installing any new software. You have a decent word-processor, a couple of reasonable graphics packages, a Web browser and e-mail program, applications for capturing, viewing and manipulating images, video and audio, and more.

When you are ready to take the next step, head for your local computer store and browse through the software. There may not be very much choice in 'serious' software – Word, Excel, Access and others in the Microsoft Office suite have become the standard business applications – but there is a huge range beyond this. The shelves are stacked with games, educational software, music and multimedia editors, home and garden designers and planners, programming language packages, plus many specialist programs for professionals and hobbyists. Before you buy, make sure that the software is XP-compatible – some of the older stuff may well not be!

And don't forget, if you want some help in learning how to use your new software, there may be a *Teach Yourself* book about it. There are *Teach Yourself* books on the main Office applications – Word, Excel, Access and PowerPoint; on several aspects of the Internet, including HTML and Web publishing; and on computer programming in C++, Java and JavaScript.

index